HOW TO
WALK A
PIG

HOW TO WALK A PIG

and other lessons in country living

STEVEN COFFMAN

LYONS & BURFORD,
PUBLISHERS

Printed in the United States of America

Design by Kathy Kikkert

10 9 8 7 6 5 4 3 2 1

Library of Congress Cataloging-in-Publication Data
Coffman, Steven.
  How to Walk a pig: and other lessons in country living / Steven Coffman.
      p.   cm.
  ISBN 1-55821-377-5 (cloth); ISBN 1-55821-488-7 (paperback)
  1. Farm Life—New York (State)—Dundee Region. 2. Family farms—New York (State)—Dundee Region. 3. Kauffman family. 1. Title.
S521.5.N7C64   1995
974.7'82—dc20
[B]   94-44392
                                                        CIP

For Bobbie, Zack and Annie, and all the friends, neighbors, family and critters who have sojourned with us on this lovely piece of land

CONTENTS

HOW TO
WALK A
PIG

PROLOGUE:
THE FARM

In the late summer of 1972, we moved from Ann Arbor, Michigan, to a sparse rural area in the Finger Lakes region of western New York, me driving a 20-foot Ryder rental truck full of our worldly goods, Bobbie alternately leading and following in our beat-up '64 Buick Electra, her with nine-month-old Zack, his traveling necessities and our neurotic old cat Jason.

We'd both cut our hair for the trip, looking almost as we had when we'd first met six years before, despite all that had changed. In Ann Arbor, my kinky black hair had grown out like a bushy silhouette of asparagus fronds (the only time in my life my hair had ever been remotely "fashionable"). I'd cut it because I didn't want to affront our new country neighbors before we even got a chance to know them. Bobbie had cut her hair more for summer coolness and style—its walnut brown flow shaped in full bangs across her forehead, following the line of her high cheekbones and oval plain-framed glasses, feathering in downy tufts across the tops of her ears and lovely neck, the tufts brushed prematurely with gray.

"Little wings—I hate them!" she berated herself. "Every time I cut my hair, I end up with these stupid little wings!"

I liked them. Just as I liked the strawberry birthmark that splotched the right side of her neck, arm and shoulder. I especially admired the way that she wore the birthmark as just a natural part of who she was, not needing to make it into either beauty mark or blemish, never giving the least thought to concealing it.

Her forthrightness and joyful buoyancy hadn't changed a bit. Nonetheless, our dreams and plans had veered dramatically, from expressway to blue-line back road. We'd both always been city people, me from South Bend and Bobbie from Detroit. When first married, our dream had still been to live in San Francisco or New York, or maybe in some large vital college town. We'd hardly considered anything else. I was a burgeoning playwright; Bobbie was working on her doctorate in psycholinguistics—a playwright had to live near theaters, and psycholinguistics was hardly the kind of field where one could simply put up one's shingle.

But then, in the spirit of those times, we more and more found ourselves lured by nature and the quest to find our place in it. Our country rides became longer and longer. We began picking shaggy manes and puffballs on a nearby golf course, stalking wild asparagus on abandoned railroad tracks, even trying to grow corn and tomatoes at the end of the oil-soaked gravel parking lot behind one of our apartments.

When two of our friends, Fritz and Mary, moved to the boonies of Maine and sent us back pictures of their garden and pet pig, we were so vicariously green that we began devouring Strout catalogs and United Farm Agency printouts that described "farmettes," "handyman specials" and "gorgeous rural acreage." By the time we helped our friends Ransom and Rosie move to a little farm outside of Nixa, Missouri, and watched their two small daughters Phaedra and Nicole playing barefoot in the barn and the creek, we knew we wanted that for our children, too.

Bobbie was pregnant with Zack when we camped from Michigan to Maine looking for affordable farmland. Our greatest surprise was the beautiful rolling hills of rural New York, the land prices almost as cheap as in interior Maine. The following June, after Bobbie had received a teaching offer from Keuka College, we made a second trip to Yates County and began looking in earnest, staring at the ancient wiring, plumbing and foundations of twenty or thirty former farmhouses, tasting the water, poking in corners and basements, trying to fit one of these dilapidated structures to our meager skills, modest budget and expansive dreams.

One of the "farms" (which hadn't actually been a working farm for about ten years) belonged to Ed and Vera Dombroski. Ed told us he'd tried unsuccessfully to sell it several times before, explaining that he'd already ruined one kidney from all his bouncing on tractors, and it still hadn't been enough for him to make a living without also having to work a full night shift in the boiler room down at Corning Glass, an hour's drive there and back.

Being city people, the first thing we looked at was the house, which Ed hardly seemed to care about at all. The rambling two-story farmhouse was built solidly, but very rough: no electricity in the bathroom or heat upstairs; no insulation in any of the walls; a cave-damp dirt-floor basement that—along with the warped, unpainted clapboard siding—housed an amazing array of rodents, wasps, spiders, reptiles, even a few amphibians.

Yet, outside, the porchlessly utilitarian structure had its amenities: the house framed by forsythias and wild rose bushes, the front yard well shaded by a wild cherry tree, an enormous white ash, and a very old but still vital sugar-pear tree whose branches spread out like tresses of gray-streaked hair, its trunk curving and thickening to broad heart-shaped hips; this pear tree reminded me of a marvelously mature woman . . . not ostentatious, but free-spirited and full of whimsical charm, who would, season by season, be filling her hair with bolts of white flowers, luscious golden baubles, clacking icy dreadlocks, and pillows of snow.

While it was just a tree, because of its place directly in front of the house, it was also a vivacious greeting . . . an example of how I hoped *we* would age.

After he dutifully showed us the house, Ed Dombroski took us for a long walk over the land, pointing out the various fallen and falling-down outbuildings: horse barn buried under brambles, turkey house half-collapsed, maple-sugar shack weathered but still solid, two large machine sheds—one needing a new roof, the other needing a new everything, and especially the old barn that was still square, despite the gaping holes in its weathered siding.

Clearly, Ed had more feelings for the barn than for the house. After pulling a few weeds at the base of the lower barn door and screeching it open on its rusty pulley, he hesitated for a moment to stare into its haunted emptiness, his memories mixing with the pungency of old manure and spoiled hay stuck in cracks between the hand-hewn rafters.

As soon as we ducked in through the wide, low doorway, we instantly had to duck again because of the dozen or so careening barn swallows that startled and thrilled us with their acrobatic darting and electric . . . *eep eep* . . . warnings as they flashed past our shoulders and faces.

"Just swallows," Ed murmured, showing us their numerous mud nests attached to the sides of the split-tree joist beams.

Ed's attention was fixed on the old rusted stanchions and the long-neglected milkhouse. Reaching up to the slanting crotch of a pegged beam, he took down a three-legged plank-top milking stool that he had used as a boy. With a musty sigh, he petted a skinny calico barn cat named Party Girl that came up to him on top of a stanchion rail.

In contrast to the dank and musty smell of the lower barn, the upper barn was full of light and space and the warm patina glow of old wood. The dry hay dust that we kicked up glittered like tiny diamond flecks in the shafts of sunlight angling down through the broken-board spaces and the small hayloft window near the peak of the cathedral-like ceiling—the same holes that the flock of pigeons had fluttered madly out of, abandoning their rafter roosts as soon as we'd climbed the grass slope and stepped into the top section of the barn.

"Still in pretty good shape. Might be you could use it for something," Ed said with another kind of sigh, sure that whatever it was we might be wanting this place for it wasn't going to be for farming.

At last, having shown us every structure, Ed walked us over every field and boundary of the 129 rolling acres of this land that his family had farmed for parts of three generations. Actually, he seemed to be showing it off to us more than trying to sell it. As we pushed through the thigh-high midsummer weeds—fields that he still referred to as cornfields, potato fields and pastures, but that now were rolling waves of mixed grasses and wildflowers, brambles and tiny trees—he rambled on about tiling springs, clearing trees by hand, pulling stumps with horses and ropes. He showed us the stump fences that still stood, as did the huge rockpiles that he had once hauled by hand into the hedgerows.

Ed loved the land; he just couldn't stand it anymore: couldn't stand farming it—barely breaking even for all that work; and couldn't stand *not* farming it, the barn empty except for memories . . . the fields fallow and less farmable each year.

When we expressed our delight at the multitude of tiny maples, knee-high oaks and shagbark hickories, Ed muttered, "Goddarn little trees—took my father and uncles most of two years to clear these fields, usin' horses and chains. These're already mostly too big t' bush-hog anymore. Darn little oaks got roots t' go down twice as far as they are high!"

We certainly had sympathy for the depth of Ed's feelings (which seemed to go down at least twice as far as *he* was high); yet turning a piece of open land back to wild hardwood forest was exactly what we had in mind.

As we walked, we saw two woodchucks, a red-tailed hawk, a flock of crows in the skeletal branches of a giant dead elm. We scared up a ruffed grouse—which stopped our hearts as it whirred up in a panic practically from our feet. We saw a doe and her fawn—bounding from field to field down the long slope of the back section, their two white tails rising and falling in tandem as we watched them recede and disappear into the lower woods.

Long before the two-hour walk brought us back to the house, Bobbie and I had exchanged enough grins and wide-eyed looks to know that—*God willin' an' the crick don't rise*—we were home.

After a bit of obligatory dickering (we asked that the old upright piano in the house and some stacked lumber in the barn be included), we agreed to the asking price of $29,500, which was a good buy even in those days. And Ed seemed to think it was a good deal for them too.

· 1 ·

TRANSITIONAL CATS

Neither Bobbie nor I had any rural roots in our knowable family histories. Unless you counted Pete and Stina, the Swedish immigrant parents of Bobbie's Uncle Arnold, who had a few farm animals near Blue Lake where Bobbie's family used to go on vacation. Or unless you counted my Grandpa Abe, who, as a Jewish immigrant from Lithuania, had built up his junkyard business by driving his horse and wagon across Michigan's countryside buying scrap iron from farmers.

Our experiences with animals had been entirely ordinary. Growing up, we'd both had family dogs, a fish in a bowl, an aunt with cats, and a couple of bouts with turtles (mostly lasting about as long as bouts with the mumps or chicken pox— although Bobbie told me she did have one turtle named Trumpcho, a Bulgarian word for "clumsy" that Bobbie's mother had also often used for her, that lasted for over a year, and that even went with them to Blue Lake in its own little pan of water.)

When Bobbie and I met during our first year in graduate school, Bobbie had already been cohabiting with Jason for several months. Jason was of that all-too-common subspecies: *felis cattus campus*—a campus cat abandoned by another student at some semester's end. Bobbie herself had just returned to Ann Arbor after two years and an abandoned marriage in Athens, Greece; and when this homeless, Persiany-bluish wanderer had come meowing in through her apartment window, she'd taken it in and called it Jason, retaining the name even after she discovered its female gender. Jason was not much of a pet, though. Typical of the subspecies, it stayed for the food and shelter, but had little capacity for affection. Traumatized by its previous abandonment and street-life travails, it spent most of its days hiding warily under couch or bed, saving most of its functioning for around 4:00 A.M.

Six years later, when it had finally come time for us to leave Ann Arbor and head out for our new life on the farm, everything had been packed, except Jason, who—in the turmoil of moving—had become even skitsier than usual. In fact, no sooner did Bobbie bring the travel box into view than the old gray thing bolted out of an open window.

Outside . . . no sign of Jason . . . no reply to Bobbie's most coaxing and mewing calls. This with twelve hours of tandem driving ahead of us in the late-August swelter, hardly an auspicious augury for our nearer-to-nature initiation. At last, after about an hour's delay, Bobbie finally managed to corner her—stuff her clawing and keening body into the travel box, load the box and Zack into our old Buick—and we were off.

The year before, we'd gotten this car in mint condition from my Aunt Florence and driven it all the way up from West Virginia, only then to have it stolen off a Detroit street: stripped, ransacked and left as car carrion in the yard of a burned-out house on the East Side. Necessity alone had emboldened me to face down the hostile "neighbors" who kept muttering, asking me what I thought I was doing . . . as I put in a battery; installed an ignition; replaced the ripped-out backseat; picked up from the mud a few possibly salvageable items like Bobbie's psychology textbooks and Zack's flattened stroller; then mounted four "new" junkyard-rimmed retreads, before limping the poor battered heap back to Ann Arbor.

You could almost say that the powder blue Buick and Jason were soulmates—the car groaning and rattling in its semi-repaired condition, Jason maintaining her terrorized moaning agony all the way from Washtenaw County, Michigan to Yates County, New York.

Upon arrival, thrilled but exhausted, we unpacked nothing but Zack's crib, the cat box, and our own mattress which we moved no farther than the living-room floor.

I don't remember what Jason did that first night, but overall she adapted no better to the country than she did to town—spending most of the next seven years as a crotchety, neurotic house cat who lived most of her days hiding under our bed, at night peeing on the houseplants as often as in the cat box, and otherwise proving that she was alive by clawing the furniture or occasionally leaving a half-dead bird, bat or mouse on our pillow. Like her namesake, Jason was indeed a wayfarer, but not exactly of heroic qualities.

On the other hand, Party Girl was as "country" as a cat could be. Inasmuch as barn cats were widely considered to belong less to a person than to a place, when the Dombroskis left the farm for a house in nearby Dundee, Party Girl stayed with the farm, spending most of her time in the barn where she hunted and received frequent itinerant toms—which was why Vera Dombroski had named her "Party Girl."

She was a small and pretty calico and, while we certainly had nothing against her, she rarely interacted with us. We were never quite sure of our responsibilities toward her. "Oh, she just stays in the barn; you don't need to do anything for her. She's just a barn cat," Vera told us in that jolly, offhand way of hers. We liked the idea of having a barn cat, not only for the pleasure of dealing with her when we went to the barn, but also for whatever rodent control she was able to provide. Of course, as this had not been a working farm for all these years, the rodent population was not exactly rampant. We guessed that Vera had probably put out cat food for her, too, and so did we— sometimes on the porch stoop and sometimes in the barn. Most of the time, though, she just left it, preferring to fend for herself. Once in a while she came up to the house, but even then she seldom came up to us or let us pet her. At some point she left; we never even knew exactly when. We felt guilty about it, though. She represented our first contact with an animal in our new environment, and we felt as if we'd failed. At least until we saw Vera Dombroski in town one day. When she asked about Party Girl, with sad embarrassment we told her the truth.

"Well, don't feel bad. It's certainly not your fault," Vera said. "Actually, I kind of expected it. I guess I shoulda told you that. I'd considered maybe keeping her with us; but, wherever she is, she's a lot better off than she'da been in town. Don't worry—she's probably already in some working barn down in the valley. Which is where I'm sure Ed'd rather be, too!" She laughed. Then, with a change of thought, she shrugged and widened her button-brown eyes: "Animals are different in the country. They come and they go. You'll get used to it."

· 2 ·

STAR

After settling in, our first two goals were to complete a fieldstone fireplace before winter and get a dog. When we went down to the SPCA in Bath, what we wanted was some mongrelly kind of family farm dog.

Our only restrictions were these:

Nothing too big. Zack was just beginning to wobble a few steps, and we didn't want some big frisky thing that was going to tromp all over him.

A puppy ... to avoid another pretraumatized animal like Jason ... nothing older than a month or two.

A male. We didn't want to have to deal with puppies, and spaying a female before letting her have a litter seemed somehow cruel, especially on a farm.

A short-haired dog to minimize the mess of shedding.

Nothing with German shepherd or Doberman in it. I was prejudiced against them—in my teenage door-to-door days of selling encyclopedias and light bulbs I'd had several harrowing encounters with both breeds. Even more, I couldn't help associating them with the German Gestapo stories I'd grown up with, which I knew was hardly the fault of the dogs, but had nonetheless left me uncomfortable with them.

Perusing the kennels, we saw quite a number of nice little shorthaired male puppies that would have completed the picture perfectly—except that the astoundingly immature and unprofessional SPCA attendant insisted on taking us specially to see a particular dog named Woodchuck: a dog of six or seven months, a long-haired female that looked to be as much German shepherd as anything else.

The attendant told us how wonderfully friendly this dog was—despite having been abused and abandoned, and already having spent three weeks here in a cage. A terrible shame, we agreed, *but* . . . then she actually pleaded with us to take it because this dog had already, in fact, been kept past the prescribed limit and was scheduled for lethal injection at closing time that night.

We hated this blubbering bleeding heart for trying to blackmail our emotions, stick us for eight or ten or twelve years with a dog that we didn't want. Not only was this dog almost exactly what we didn't want; but, after all it'd been through, it was bound to be a neurotic mess besides. Let *her* take it home!

And besides, no matter which dog we chose, it was going to mean curtains for some other *un*chosen dogs. We didn't want to think about that. Every puppy in the place was cute, in desperate need, and worthy of being saved. If we'd thought we were going to feel guilty over the fate of every dog we didn't choose, we could've just gone to a kennel and bought a little purebred beagle or shorthaired terrier somewhere. Except that we knew that all those kennel dogs were considered to have value, were wanted and would somehow be taken care of, and, in the end, would be no more lovable, loyal or protective than these. The point was that we'd come to save some unwanted puppy's life and give it a wonderful home, but we also needed to find a pet that we were going to be happy with.

"That long hair's going to get all over everything," Bobbie muttered.

"Do we look like a couple of saps or something? I hate this!"

"It's already big enough to trample Zack."

"It's at least half German shepherd; look at the nose and feet. And we definitely decided on a male, didn't we?"

"Honey, we just have to look at this dispassionately, and pick out the dog that's best for us!"

On the way back from Bath, we changed Woodchuck's name to Star.

Our ultimate decision had had very little to do with the attendant's softheadedness; rather, it had been the sweet and friendly way that the lively little dog had come right up to the crosshatched cage and pressed her own case. She couldn't quite get her pointy muzzle to us, but she had certainly licked us nonetheless.

By the next summer, Star was tall as a shepherd, thick as a mastiff, and already well established as Queen of the Hill. She was as stalwart, brave and loyal as she was huge. She was also immovable . . . but not a quick learner. Our best guess was that she was about forty percent German shepherd, and equal parts collie, St. Bernard, and moose.

As to our original list of concerns, some were realized and some weren't:

Especially as a young brute, she knocked Zack regularly Oshkosh over B'Gosh—if not by jumping, then by overeager nuzzling or with her wildly wagging ropelike tail.

Not only was she impossibly big and overzealous for the house, but her long, tawny hair shed in softball-sized clumps. As a result, she very soon became an exclusively outside dog.

In fact, we did allow her to have a litter before getting her spayed, though the experience was not at all what we'd expected.

Nor did she prove to be the least bit traumatized or mean as a result of her early misfortunes or German shepherd genes.

Never once did she growl or snap at Zack—or later at *Annie* —not even when they pulled her ears, landed surprise leaps on her as if she were a sofa, pulled open her incredible jaws and stuck in hands, feet, faces . . . nor even when they hitched her to a wagon or tried to saddle her up. Her patience and ability to withstand pain and indignity were almost equal to her energy and strength.

The only ones who ever made her growl were the UPS man and Vernon, a boy who lived in the valley and often hunted up on the hill. As for the UPS man, there was just something about that big brown truck; maybe it was just the only thing bigger than she was that ever entered her territory. And Vernon threw rocks at Star . . . although, in fairness to him, that may have only been in response to the way she menaced him. I don't know what she had against Vernon. Maybe, because of his hunting, she associated him with the frightening, ear-piercing noise of gunshots. Or it may have been his smell, as woodsy and unwashed as any fur-trapping frontiersman. Basically, Vernon wore the same clothes in all seasons, the *very* same— layered vests, flannel shirts and sleeveless hunting coat—even the day after he had walked by the house with a dead possum draped around his neck like a not-quite-ermine collar.

In any case, as much as she intimidated Vernon and the UPS man, Star never actually went after them. She was, in fact, as fine a watchdog as we could have imagined—unerringly vigilant, an unignorable presence, but never threatening. What she did when we weren't there I can't say, but no one we knew ever complained; nor did we ever feel a need to put a lock on the door.

The only other time I ever saw Star menace a human was after she gave birth to her pups. My back had given out and I had been unable to get out of bed for several weeks. Bobbie told me that Star had made a den in the barn, at the base of a huge haystack that I had previously brought in by hand, or rather with scythe, pitchfork and pickup truck (undoubtedly a contributing factor to my ailing back). Not wanting to miss the event completely, I forced myself up and, stiff as a board, inched my way out to the barn.

I'd left an old wagon wheel propped up against the hay-stack, and, amazingly, Star had dug out a soft den for herself directly behind the wagon wheel. The effect was awe-inspir-ing: not only the cozy softness of the den, but its fortresslike positioning. In order to get to her pups, an invader first had to get through the spokes of the large wheel, and then they had to get through *her!* I was taking a very gentle look at the newborn pups. Behind me, Scott Kiklowitz, a very lively school friend of Zack's, came rushing into the barn without paying any respect to the situation. At that moment, my face was within inches of Star's. I was looking beyond her to the squirming still-wet puppies. Suddenly she bared her teeth and growled in a way that I didn't know. It was not meant for me and it was just a warning, but it was a warning that any living creature in the world would have respected.

Many times after that, recalling the ferocity of that instant, I wondered all the more at Star's abiding gentle sweetness and patience. Of all the animals we ever had, Star had about her the greatest sense that she could have been at home in the wild. When she showed up in the front yard with a groundhog or a hunter-discarded deer's head in her jaws, it amazed me that she also tried so hard to do our bidding. Simply put, it was the realization that she didn't stay with us for food and shelter, but for love.

· 3 ·

THE CASE OF THE MISSING CHICKEN

When Star ate, she was gusto incarnate. The world stood back! There was almost nothing that she wouldn't eat, except maybe fruits, lettuce, and occasionally a potato. She was the ultimate organic recycler. Spoiled milk, give it to Star. Green cheese, she'll love it. Moldy bread. Leftover spaghetti. Anything that even smacked of fat, gristle or bone. When Star took on a soup bone or shank bone, she didn't gnaw on it but crushed it, and when she was finished there was nothing left to bury.

At first we tried to be careful about what we gave her—until the famous "Missing Chicken Incident."

Bobbie had invited for dinner three favorite former students from her Psychology of Women class. They helped us put up an oak crossbeam to shore up a worrisome sag that had remained over our heads since I'd innocently knocked out a load-bearing wall in our "opening up" of the farmhouse's downstairs. The new oak beam was extremely heavy and hard for the women to hold up while I wedged it in place . . . making us all feel some combination of "gender liberated" and *macho*. We celebrated in freewheeling 60s style. By the time we started getting serious about dinner, we were all feeling a little silly and absentminded anyway, and it got to be pretty much of a joke when we couldn't find the chicken. Bobbie was quite sure she'd left it on the kitchen table, but it wasn't there now, nor in the refrigerator or oven, nor in the pantry or living room, in cupboards or upstairs, in basement or bathroom. In fact, it wasn't in the house.

Regardless of our frame of mind, we knew perfectly well that we had left a whole large 2½- or 3-pound chicken to defrost on the kitchen table. We ended up having something else for dinner, and the missing chicken was still an unsolved mystery when we shut down for the night.

We weren't thinking of Star because we never let her in the

house. Even if she had managed to sneak in with the guests, it could only have been for a few seconds before we would have ordered her back out, and certainly we would have noticed if she'd had a whole chicken in her mouth. Nonetheless, in those few seconds that she'd been in the kitchen, she had in fact wolfed down—*inhaled*—the chicken whole, something that we didn't discover until the next morning when she upchucked the semidigested mess.

Prior to this episode, we'd always been very careful not to give Star chicken bones. We'd heard that they could easily splinter and puncture a dog's innards. But then it struck us that she'd never had the least problem with the frequent ground-hogs, rabbits, squirrels and deer parts that she brought into the yard—mostly carrion that came off the road or the leavings of hunters. We knew that she also caught groundhogs and an occasional dreamy rabbit, all of which she ate with great relish and digested perfectly well. In fact, before this 3-pound chicken that she'd taken in a single gulp, none of it had ever brought forth more than a healthy burp. Following this assessment of her amazing digestive abilities, we were less careful about giving her chicken bones, or anything else short of roofing nails.

· 4 ·

WILD GEESE

The first time the geese came over, we'd been on the farm only for a little over a month. It was mid-September and dramatic changes were everywhere at hand: The week before, we'd had a killing frost and, overnight, nearly every flower, cultivated or wild, had gone brown and flat. The trees were beginning to change and were poised to ignite into a breathtaking blaze of incandescent color. As if nature were suddenly spiking all its energy levels up into the red zone, birds swirled in huge flocks, deer dashed unexpectedly into the road, and squirrels stuffed their cheeks with a panicky sense of purpose.

Nothing, though, was more dramatic than the geese.

I was in back of the shed splitting and stacking firewood. Before seeing them, I heard them but didn't know what I was hearing: a steady yipping in the distance that at first sounded like a pack of dogs. Unlike dogs, though, the sound had a soul-stirring cadence, a modulated throbbing that, for a moment, reminded me of some Apache chanting I'd once heard in Arizona. Leaning on my ax, cocking an ear, I realized that the sound was coming from the sky—and was also gradually becoming louder and more distinct. It was only when my eye and ear met at the wide sweep of the unmistakable V-formation that I hurried into the house and yelled for Bobbie to come out quick.

It was something we'd seen dozens of times in *Natural History* and on nature documentaries, but not in life, and never veering toward us. We watched in amazement as the honking V steadily pulsed overhead, the lead goose with its neck straight out, its hard beak piercing the wind, the fifty or so other giant birds splaying off in two straight lines behind it—one off its left wing, the other from its right—forming the powerfully sleek arrowhead that seemed to slice open a piece of sky for them to fly through. In our excitement, we grabbed hold of each other, watching silently until the flock had passed over in its relentless southerly pursuit and disappeared into the horizon, the primal sound trailing off like rumbling thunder after the lightning flash was gone.

And yet, that first fall, as much as we loved seeing the geese and responded viscerally to their pull—and were madly enthusiastic to jump into everything rural with both feet—we didn't quite yet have a feel for the dance. Seeing them fly over was a thrill, and the next spring when they flew over again coming north it was another thrill, but these were still detached events, not yet integrated into the rhythm of our lives.

Sometimes they flew over us so low that we could hear the beating of their wings. Sometimes we watched them struggling into impossible headwinds, seeming to make no progress at all, again and again changing leaders and tack—the flock opening up to let the old leader rest within the protection of the V while another less-fatigued bird came forward to assume the lead—before, at last, they managed to inch forward and pull away. Sometimes we imagined them having risen from some pristine Canadian lake, their wings already having pumped for a thousand miles with another thousand or so miles yet to go, and wondered at how indomitable and how in sync with the driving ebb-and-flow forces of the earth they were.

But it took us quite a few seasons, many quickening autumns and regenerating springs, before we realized that the geese were not only part of the spring and fall, but were on their cutting edge—nature's vanguard—trumpeting heralds proclaiming that summer was gone and winter was in the air, that another winter was on the run and long live the spring. In September, the earliest-turning sumacs and sugar maples seemed to wave red flags to urge them on; in early April, their northbound magnetism seemed to pull the snowbells and crocuses up out of the slushy earth.

We began to to take tremendous heart from their spring appearance, and to feel not just a thrill but also a note of sadness in their autumnal calling. Eventually, before hearing or seeing them, we began to anticipate their coming, as if they had become so insinuated into our internal rhythm that our changes were also marked by their seasonal flights.

· 5 ·

CLUSTER FLIES AND INDIAN SUMMER

The first time my mother and father came to see the farm, it was Indian summer and should have been glorious. The way they say it around here is that you can't have Indian summer until you've had squaw winter, meaning a killing frost. Never mind the naïve racist and sexist overtones of that, the idea still stood as one of munificent reprieve: one required a foretaste of winter . . . before being fully able to appreciate such precious extra days of easy comfort and afterglow.

Early October. Trees and fields gorgeous with autumn color. Temperature over eighty! As if the gods were smiling in special consideration of this delicate and probably difficult visit.

My parents were not country people. They were small-city people: my mother from Grand Rapids, my father from South Bend. Their thirty-five years of marriage started off in Cincinnati before returning to South Bend. Even though South Bend existed within the farm state of Indiana, it had always been essentially industrial, more of a miniature Chicago or Detroit than an overgrown Kokomo or Terre Haute.

Except for an orchestrated visit here and there, my parents had never even been on a farm. They had been brought up with middle-class small-city ways that had eventually segued into middle-class suburban ways. Their professionally decorated house was kept meticulously clean, its outside consisting of trimmed shrubs, carefully weeded flower beds, and a neatly mowed lawn. They kept no pets. And if any insect or critter got into the house, everything stopped until it was chased out, or preferably killed and disposed of.

They were not especially happy about our move to the farm. They didn't understand it—in the same way that they hadn't understood my long hair. They loved us dearly and had never pressured us to live close by, despite a sadness at being so far from Zack, who was still their only grandchild. They understood our desire to try someplace new, as they themselves had started out in Cincinnati. But they didn't understand the limitations of a country well and septic system, or why we had no electricity in the bathroom. They didn't understand why an urbanized, college-educated young couple with a toddler would mortgage themselves to a defunct farm. And they certainly didn't understand insects in the house.

We thought the Indian summer might be like a spoonful of honey, making things more palatable. We didn't even know what cluster flies were. Yet, just as Indian summer brought humans out of their houses to luxuriate in this late dividend of unexpected summer, so there was also a great stirring in the woods and fields, each kind using the extra warmth in its own way. Woodchucks basking beside their holes. Birds and squirrels chasing after each other garrulously, as if nature had leapfrogged winter all the way to spring. Wasps and bees actively buzzing about, despite the absence of flowers to draw nectar from. And cluster flies—which, unbeknownst to us, had already taken up winter residence in our house, having crept in through every crack and seam during squaw winter—now, by the thousands, suddenly seeking to get back *out!*

In appearance, cluster flies (*Pollenia rudis*) might easily be mistaken for house flies; in behavior, however, cluster flies were hardly like them at all. They didn't land on food, zip from room to room, or crawl all over clothes and skin—cluster flies came inside to hibernate. (While we were later often told that they laid their eggs in the walls, in fact their eggs are laid in the ground, where they become earthworm parasites, thus damaging the gardener's "best friend" as well as the gardener's *sanity.*)

What made cluster flies so exasperating was not only their massing numbers, but also that—in seeking to *un*hibernate whenever the weather warmed—they flocked to every window . . . turning every lovely view into a nauseating crawl of frustrated buzzing . . . until out of—*Starvation? Window madness? Insect senility?*—they precipitately turned into whirling upside-down dervishes, suddenly rising and then dropping dead on our floor . . . dead on our bed . . . dead in our food . . . dead on our heads.

Our old house was so porous, that it was a living laboratory

for the "successful invasion/unsuccessful mass exodus" phenom-
enon. We tried leaving the windows open, but as many flies
came in as went out (as did a number of yellow jackets and
wasps). We vacuumed them up, but others endlessly took their
place. We even tried spraying them, but that just quickened
their death dance and left them spinning and buzzing on the
floor in greater and noisier numbers.

This coming of Indian summer had not been a smile of the
gods, but a trickster's prank. Wilted by the unexpected heat, my
parents had brought no summer clothes, only fall clothes—
sweaters, coats, heavy slacks. While Zack played by himself on
the adjoining living-room floor, we all sat in range of a clunky
fan we'd set up on the kitchen counter, sat on our wobbly,
auction-begotten, pattern-back chairs, sat opposite each other
around our heavy mogul-legged, round oak table . . . as though
stumped in failed negotiation and waiting for some mediator.

And as much as the heat enervated my parents, the cluster
flies sapped their spirits. The buzzing was so distracting that we
could hardly follow each other's conversation. In semishock,
trying as hard as they could not to notice, Mom and Dad sat
stiffly posed in their double-knit neatness: their hands folded
in front of them, their faces like lacquered fans—painted and
firmly spread with looks of brittle and brutal *pleasantness.* Bobbie
and I squirmed about, trying to do something to make up for
what we couldn't undo.

"Should we go for a walk?"

"It's too hot for that, I'm afraid."

"Maybe we should play some cards—we could play a little bridge."

"No, I don't think so."

Bobbie put up some coffee and brought out a small pear cake that she'd made. "From our own pears," she sang with a note of exaggerated pride as she cut Dad the first big piece.

"Mm, we both love pears," Mom said.

But just as Dad picked up his fork, a buzzing cluster fly dropped right onto the piece of pear cake, spinning on its back and beginning its final death throes only three or four unignorable inches from his bending-forward face.

"*Ugh!*" Bobbie burst out. "These *f— stupid* flies, I HATE them!" She quickly grabbed the dish and cake from under Dad's nose, swept the piece of cake and still-buzzing fly into the compost bucket under the sink and came back with a clean plate. "I'm so embarrassed, Dad—here, let me get you a fresh piece."

"Uh, no, thanks," Dad replied curtly.

"But, dear, you love pears—these are the kids' own pears," Mom tried.

"I don't want any. How can I *eat?*"

Why couldn't Mother Nature have just dropped a tornado on us instead of feigning summer kindness and then hitting us with this humiliating dignity-effacing Sartrean plague, this curse of Oedipus and Orestes?

All else having failed, we turned to Zack—our progeny, my parents' first grandchild, sole bearer of the Coffman name into the next generation. There he was, just two weeks before his first birthday, so happily crawling about the living-room floor in nothing but his Pampers, pushing his ding-dong ball and musical giraffe. Suddenly, rolling to a sitting position, he looked at us with his huge brown eyes and gave us a laughing smile that showed us his mouthful of dead flies that began drooling down his precious chin.

A horrible fight flared up between my father and me that intensified until my parents ended up leaving for a nearby motel, leaving me boiling with frustration and Bobbie in tears. After the visit, letters of accusation and recrimination were exchanged between father and son. Followed by letters of contriteness and apology. And finally, the next spring in South Bend, with Zack sparkling clean and neat as a pin in those pristine surroundings, my father and I laid it to rest. I told him of our plans to tighten up the house with new siding and insulation. The cluster flies were not mentioned, but the clear implication was that we had *not* simply accepted them as a "natural" part of our lives. And Dad said if we needed any help, he'd be glad to give us a loan that we could pay back whenever we were able. I accepted the offer gratefully, not only because we needed it, but even more for the gesture ... for the accommodating acceptance of our differing points of view.

· 6 ·
A HOG I—PIG IRONIES

At least we hadn't gotten the pig until after my parents' visit. It had never been a question of whether we wanted a pig; the only question was if the pig was going to be pork or a pet—a question we'd been weighing since our two years in Iowa City from '67 to '69 . . . in the rising and falling heart of the sixties, a time when "pignification" was as changeable as the times . . . pig repute running the gamut from an odious symbol of unconscionable greed, aggression and moral abomination (slum landlords, racist cops, warmongering politicians) . . . to an endearing flesh-and-blood-symbol of what was variously real, unpretentious, very pretentious, ugly-but-true-blue, not-pretty-but-cute, historically underappreciated and misunderstood—these various incarnations being represented, for instance, by:

Ken Kesey's Hog Farm

The Yippee Nomination of Pigasus for Prez

Miss Piggy

Andy Warhol's "Pretty as a Pigture" poster (a 24 x 30 copy of which we brought from Ann Arbor to the farm)

Police *embracing* the appellation, even staging Kids vs. Pigs softball games

The Washington Redskins Offensive Line calling themselves "The Hogs"

A national run on Arkansas Razorback pighead "hawg" hats

Pigs were in the air.

And while, to some extent, we were also caught up in this porcine revisionism (we were certainly a lot more comfortable with *A Hog on Ice* than with "OFF THE FUCKING PIGS!"), it was the down-to-earth animal itself that really captured our fancy, the adorable tiny piglets that crowded the fences on our spring drives on Iowa backroads; the pet pig of Mary and Fritz, our Michigan friends who had preceded our country move by buying a rugged little chunk of interior Maine.

Actually, Bobbie's love may have gone even farther back, to the days of Pooh's Piglet and Charlotte's Wilbur. In any case—in those first days on the farm—there was a time when I think she was truly serious about wanting us to have a *house* pig.

By that time, she had clipped numerous articles, serious and semiserious accounts of pig intelligence, friendliness, loyalty, honesty, even *cleanliness*—as though any ordinary pig would have made a perfect Boy Scout. Indeed, pigs were said to be much cleaner than cows, horses, sheep, chickens or dogs. In fact, given the opportunity, pigs always reserved specific areas for their excretory functions. Was it a pig's fault that its proclivity for cleanliness was undermined so often by impossibly cramped and overcrowded conditions? As to a pig's penchant for rolling in mud . . . that was its only means of keeping cool in hot weather (God—for unknown reasons of His own—not having equipped pigs with the ability to pant or sweat!)

The house-pig idea was like a whimsical debate that kept threatening to assume actual shape. There was something gloriously outlandish about it. Would a pig lie peacefully beside the blazing hearth? Would it wag its curly tail when we said "That's a good pig!" or some other cooing inanity? Would it bring me my moccasins to get a casual scratch behind the ears?

Were we serious? As I recall, we were serious enough to consider several drawbacks. Could we reasonably ask a friend or neighbor to take care of our pig if we left town? What would it do to Star for her to know that we let a pig stay in the house but not her? As much fun as a piglet or young pig might be, what would we do when it grew into a 200- or 300-pound sow or full-size boar?

This last point ended the house-pig discussion and also led us to the more serious question of whether we were getting this pig simply to enjoy it and learn about it—or for meat. Clearly, for any purpose, including meat, we were obligated to provide it with good care, but not with the same attitude and affection. We couldn't possibly slaughter and eat a pet. Nor "put it down" simply because it got too big and was less "cute" than it had once been.

On the other hand: Were we willing to take care of a full-grown hog to the end of its natural days? Which also begged the broader question: Was our farm merely to be a flower-child's playground, or were we serious about trying to live a more down-to-earth country life?

Finally—soberly—we decided that raising a pig for food was something that would be good for us to do, our guide being *The Foxfire Book*, an unsentimental view of self-sufficiency, in which pigs were very useful in the art of hardscrabble survival.

Of course, no amount of seriousness could obscure the irony, in light of my Jewish upbringing, that our first farm animal was going to be a pig.

· 7 ·

AHOG II—HOW TO WALK A PIG

Vernon's family had pigs. This family, about a country mile down our hill into Crystal Valley, originally hailing from somewhere in rural Connecticut, had accents that seemed . . . half-Appalachian/half-Acadian? . . . eighteenth-century Welsh peasant? . . . anyway, like nothing else we'd ever heard before.

Except for a few casual incidents and necessary inter-actions, these folks kept pretty much to themselves, and so did we. About all we knew for sure was that the whole family— wife, two sons, four daughters and at least some of the animals—lived together in some kind of arrangement in a roofed-over basement that had only slits for windows and no interior walls. Besides their pigs, they had chickens, a dog or two, and at least one cow. As far as we could tell, their entire survival depended upon the subsistence farming of their fifteen or twenty uphill acres.

Mostly, we only saw them when they were out walking to Dundee—our nearest town—five hilly miles away and a pretty good hike, especially in bad weather with an armful of groceries. When the father was still around, we used to see them at least once or twice a week, always walking in the same configuration: father first, then eldest son, second son, eldest daughter, second daughter, third daughter, fourth daughter, mother bringing up the rear—eyes straight ahead, walking single file on the shoulder of the road. A couple times, in bad weather, we stopped to ask if we could give them a ride or get something for them, but the father, always gave us this painfully broad smile, just said, "No thankee," and resumed walking, the whole brood filing past us without as much as a look . . . except for the mother who always managed a haggard smile of what we took to be neighborly gratitude for our stopping to ask.

Sometime early in that first fall, very soon after we had gotten Star, we walked down to their covered-basement dwelling and asked the father if he'd be interested in selling us a pig. "Sure, suppose I could do that," he said, always maintaining that unsettlingly brittle grin. There was no question of haggling. For fifty dollars we bought a year-old neutered male Hampshire already named Ahog, which we thought was the best name for a pig we'd ever heard.

To get Ahog, I thought I'd have to borrow a truck, but the eldest son just grinned and laughed.

"Why'd'nt y'jus walk it home? Rope'n stick's all y' need! I git'm for y'."

When he returned and handed me about eight or ten feet of rope, I didn't know what I was doing, so I made a slipknot and started to tie it around the pig's neck, the way you would with a dog.

"Noee, not ataway!"

Sure enough, as soon as I tightened the noose, Ahog pulled right out of it—because its bristly skin was surprisingly slick; and because of the way its head tapered from neck to snout, my slipknot worked about as well as tightening a collar on a slippery funnel.

"Yay way; I'll showee how . . ."

Though it was hard to tell, my guess was that the boy was maybe seventeen or eighteen because he had the beginning scruff of a beard and a few long chin hairs. His teeth had already gone bad, and, like Vernon, he looked like he was going to wear his clothes until they molted. He did, however, know how to walk a pig. "See'ere . . ." He put my slipknot around one of the pig's back legs, down low between its knobby hock and cleft hoof, and pulled it tight. "If'ee don be wantin t' go, poke'm a good one lack'iss."

He demonstrated by giving the pig a sharp poke in its side with the stick and, sure enough, after squealing its annoyance, the pig headed down the road. After just a few steps, though, it veered to the shoulder and commenced chomping the lower leaves of some flowering chicory.

"If'ee ain be goin lackee wish'm to, see'ere . . . " the boy said, and, with that, jerked the taut rope on its rear leg, plopping the pig flat down on its thick jowls. It indignantly snorted: "Oownkkkk!"—then immediately scrambled back up onto its stubby legs.

So, that was *it* . . . how to walk a pig?

I just thought it an unnecessarily mean and nasty trick. I got Ahog moving down the road, hardly needing anything more than a little gentle urging to get him headed in exactly the right direction.

The whole thing seemed pricelessly quaint and funny. Not just the amazing transaction and the starry wonderment of who our neighbors were—right here in the middle of New York State, only an hour from Cornell "on its lofty knoll"—but *me*, Jewish kid from Studebaker town, walking home my very own pig . . . not actually *walking* as much as tiptoe-jogging . . . Ahog so nicely tripping along, me just trying to give him all the slack I could.

But then suddenly the pig made a surprisingly quick rush for the bushes. Except for my slyly applied tether, he'd have been gone for sure. As it was, he was two legs into the culvert when the rope went taut and the pig went flat. I had to get into the ditch and poke him with the stick to get him up and on the road again. Variations on this theme recurred three or four times more before he finally sized up the situation, and then nicely walked me up the hill and the rest of the way home.

· 8 ·

AHOG III—YOU'VE GOT TO SMILE (WITH A KNIFE IN YOUR TEETH)

We did not allow ourselves to love Ahog. He was a fine animal and we surely loved the fact of him, but because we knew the inevitable outcome of our relationship, it was important not to let ourselves get too close. We treated him well. I converted the maple-sugar shack into a pig house, building him a good-sized pen, using locust splits for the posts and oak saplings for rails. I also built him a large trough in which he could make a perfect pig of himself with the daily slop mix of garbage, water, and vitamin-supplemented pig chow. He got that every morning, and every night, as a (fattening) treat, we gave him a coffee can or two of cracked corn.

As Bobbie's articles had predicted, the pig proved to be reasonably even-tempered and "clean," at least to the extent that it reserved one corner of its pen for excretory functions. As far as intelligence went, Ahog certainly recognized us individually, knew when mealtime was, and got excited when he saw us coming. Truthfully, if he was smarter than that, we didn't want to know.

In winter, to keep him warm, we filled the inside of the pig house with straw, which at night he buried himself in, each morning rising like a living haystack, shaking himself off and snorting while he pranced out to greet us and get his food.

For most of the fall and all of the winter, we kept him. In that time he just about doubled in size and, for those final two months, we tripled his ration of cracked corn. Our minds had long since been made up that we were going to have him slaughtered and keep the meat ourselves. It had to do with being self-sufficient and facing reality. Some visiting friends said that we should at least sell him at market and buy an anonymous pig to eat; but, while we didn't know *what* might have gone into any other pig, we *did* know that Ahog had been "corned off" and had never been sick or junked up with hormones or God-only-knew-what. A few of our old friends were shocked that we could eat our own pig, but we had our minds set philosophically. The way we saw it, to eat meat but be unable to face the death of an animal was both cowardly and hypocritical.

In the way of the Indians, we thought that what one needed to do was to treat one's quarry with respect and gratitude. *Thank you for giving me your strength; we'll try to merit the taking of it . . .*

However, thinking this way was one thing and living it out was another. Despite our intentions, about the same time that we changed Ahog's feed, we also found ourselves beginning to pull back. Not that it had ever been a pet, but now we hardly even saw it as a pig, just pork. Instead of saying "Nice pig," we were just as likely to say nothing and just think "Nice hams."

It was mid-March when we called up old Tom Trojanowski. Our friend Frank, who lived on the next road over, told us he'd used Trojanowski a few times and he'd always done a good job. Frank was a carpenter by trade but also raised his own corn and hay and beef cattle; he'd grown up on a farm and knew about such things.

It was a clear March day and I was blue as I could be. Bobbie had taken Zack to a baby-sitter and gone to work. I was holding philosophically solid, but it didn't do much to allay my queasiness when I saw Trojanowski's pickup pull into the drive.

Star immediately jumped out barking and charged to stand her ground. I hadn't even thought about Star, but clearly I didn't need her to be a part of all this. After several calls I got her over to me, led her into the woodshed, then closed her in and barred the door. This was the first time that Star had been in any way confined since we'd freed her from her death-row cage at the SPCA. Inside the woodshed she began whining piteously and scratching to get out, but I had too many other things on my mind to worry about her, too. From the beginning, Star and Ahog had been like jealous rivals, each ready to take a nip at the other's back if given the chance . . . hardly anything I wanted to deal with today.

By the time I'd dealt with the dog, Tom Trojanowski was waiting for me at the front stoop. He was a stout old country man. Like the boys we'd gotten the pig from, he was wearing many layers of jerseys and flannel shirts inside a very old pair of Carhart overalls, a torn vest over that. And yet, unlike the boys, except for his outermost layer he was quite clean. Almost inappropriately so for the job at hand. Or maybe I was just thinking that because he so unnerved me, standing there like he was, with a rifle in one hand and a little stack of Bible pamphlets in the other.

"Mornin'," he said, tucking the pamphlets under his arm and extending his hand. While I was shaking hands with him, comforted by the strength of his grip but also feeling slightly conspiratorial, he asked me if I had yet rededicated my life to Jesus Christ. When I said no, I definitely hadn't, he kind of nodded, then chuckled and gave me a kindly smile.

"Well, ain't my business to rush no one, but sometimes folks don't even realize they're right on the edge of takin' that step . . . an' just in case, I always like t' leave 'em with a little litterchure, t' just maybe help 'em with that first step t' glory."

I told him to keep the pamphlets for someone who was nearer to taking the step than I was, and he said, "Sure, yup, no problem. So, you got a hog that needs slaughterin', that right?"

I was so shaken by the juxtaposition that I almost changed my mind—but didn't. As I walked him over toward the pig house, he asked me if the hog had been fed yet today. I said it had. He asked if we'd been treating it good right up to the last.

"A lot of folks think just 'cause they're plannin' t' take a critter's life, they got no more need t' be good t' it, but the Lord give us this bounty, an' this bounty also belong t' the Lord—so it's important that we treat all critters kindly, for the innocent gifts of the Lord's that they be."

At the pig house, Ahog was extremely nervous and agitated.

"Hey, you're a good healthy critter, ain't y'? You been treated to a fine life, I see. That's a blessing." He stood behind

Ahog and somewhat calmed him by scratching him behind the ears. Then he put the rifle to that same spot and, with one not-very-loud shot, dropped the pig, which instantly buckled to its knees and fell over sideways with only one short breathy squeal.

Trojanowski immediately flipped the safety on the .22 and propped it up against the sapling rail that I had fashioned for the pig house and that now shocked me with its instant superfluity. The pig was dead now and the man no longer spoke sweetly of it, its soul presumably having departed to Hog Heaven.

Now it was just meat, and he quickly set to work. "Where's a good place to hang it?" he asked.

I didn't know anything about it, I replied. More accurately I should have said that I was green as an unripe banana, for I surely was.

He said we could hang him in the barn, but it would probably be better to dress him out on a big tree like the big ash in front of the house.

In a fog, I said, "Fine."

I knocked out the bottom rail of the pen. We each grabbed a back leg of the still-warm carcass and slid it out across the frozen ground and dragged it all the way out to the road. Several people had told us that it was much better to slaughter an animal before the weather warmed and the ground got soft, and I could already see why—so there was no mud or thick brush or swarms of flies to deal with.

At the road, the old man threw a rope over one of the big ash tree's lower limbs, wrapped the two rear legs of the carcass together and raised it by its notched hocks until it was stretched out full and off the ground, then tied it off, and unfolded a large square of plastic which he spread beneath it.

"I used t' be a drunk'n a wastrel till I found the Lord," he said, as with his glistening-sharp skinning knife he slit the animal from its anus to the point of its jaw . . . as though unzipping an overnight bag. Instantly, a gush of blood, entrails, digestive juices and feces spilled out of the open meatbag, much of it hitting the plastic, giving rise to a gasping hiss of stench and steam.

"I had one foot purt' near down the Devil's gullet when I fine'ly took that step't I'da been thinkin'd be s' hard t' take. But y' know what? Was the easiest thing I ever done, easy's a baby suckin' its momma's milk."

He scraped out the dangling innards, then began scraping the soft pink flesh from the tough bristly hide. The whole time I stood there in wordless shock, a stupid grin frozen on my face, as if I'd suffered a temporary stroke . . . as though some kind of fuse had blown and left the mechanism of my mouth and jaw fixed like that. Emotionally I was astonished, fascinated, horrified, acting in an absurdist play by Ionesco or Genet. If I moved my mouth, I was sure I'd burst out either laughing or screaming, but I didn't know which.

"A man might even think he's happy, might keep smilin' all day long, might look like he's got everything he needs," he said, setting aside the heart, liver and kidneys, wrapping up the rest of the innards in the plastic like a knapsack and tying it with a piece of baling twine, "but appearances kin deceive . . . the Devil—the Great Deceiver—he come in many pleasin' n' winsome forms. Y' know, man's gotta smile t' hold a knife in his teeth—might be smilin', but he still got that knife."

His slaughtering fee was $15 and the hide. Before letting Star out of the woodshed, I dug a hole in a far field and buried the sack of entrails. I threw several buckets of water on the spot by the road to wash some of the blood and viscous leftovers into the ditch, to disperse it and dilute the stench. Then I cut the carcass down, put it in the wheelbarrow and took it to the upper barn, where I strung it up from one of the crossbeams, putting a garbage can under it to catch most of the drippings. I'd heard that a carcass ought to hang for at least 24 hours before being butchered.

When I let Star out, she went wild, first licking the stickiness on me, then racing from one venue of action to the next, in the pigpen sniffing and licking the spot where the killing had happened, for a curious moment looking to see where Ahog was, then romping over for a little nosh under the ash tree, finally following her nose to the barn where she sniffed and yapped at the 150 pounds of fresh meat that was dangling several feet above her best jump.

We thought about butchering the pig ourselves but didn't think we were ready for that, taking it instead to a small meat locker and processing outfit in Watkins Glen. We kept all the parts, though.

Using *The Foxfire Book* —not as our Bible but as our guide— we made use of every part of the pig that we could. According to the book, the Appalachian mountain folk "used everything but the *squeal*." We didn't do quite that well, but we boiled the head for head cheese, roasted the hocks and feet, ate the heart, liver, kidneys and tongue, had the sausage stuffed in the intestinal casing, tried but couldn't stomach a soup recipe for the tail, gave suet to the birds, rendered some of the fat and molded a few primitive candles. We passed on the instructions for making soap, doubting that we could create anything we'd want to wash with. These efforts met with varying degrees of palatability and success.

The more traditional cuts of meat, however—hams, loin, ribs, chops, bacon and roast—lasted all that winter and well into the next. Whatever concern we had about any residual lachrymose flavor, it was, in fact, the tastiest pork we'd ever eaten.

· 9 ·
DEER SEASON

Out here there were five seasons: the four that Mother Nature rather unevenly and capriciously squalled, baked, slogged and teased; and one that was death-and-taxes predictable (and some would say just about as desirable)—Deer Season!

On the first morning of our first Deer Season (always a Monday in mid-November, Yates County's largest work-absentee day of the year), I thought war had broken out. I thought the Russians had come—or maybe North Vietnam or Cambodia had *really* found a way to threaten our National Security! Anyway—whatever the unlikely and perverse political underpinnings—I was sure we were under *goddamn* siege!

In the hunter's orange of predawn, we were jarred awake by a steady roar of bivouacking vehicles grinding down our country road. At the road's edge, young Star (just out of puppyhood) stood gallantly, ready to take on the invaders either one by one or all together.

With a weary glance at the glowering clock's 5:45, I was still waiting for this nightmare afterimage to pop into some reasonable perspective. As reality suddenly dawned, Bobbie coming to at the same time, I leaped into my Wolverine sweatshirt and jeans.

"What is it?" Bobbie asked with sudden alarm.

"I don't know. All hell's breaking loose out there!"

"Out *there?*"

Unbelievably, on our nameless dirt road (actually our road had four different names depending on whom you talked to, but no road sign)—we saw twenty-five or thirty pickups, most of them carrying four or five orange-vested, red-hatted, plaid-shirted *heavily armed* troops.

"Jesus, they're all hunters!" Bobbie gasped.

That was the second time we deprived Star of her freedom. This time we brought her into the house until I could get together a stake and a rope that would hold her.

It wasn't so much the idea of killing deer that bothered me. Except for their incredibly gentle grace and beauty, I might've wanted to see if I could bring one in myself. After all, deer were more than plentiful, and venison was excellent meat. What made it so disgraceful was the blood-lusting, partylike, Rambonehead way they went about it—for three weeks driving through every bush and hedgerow, subjecting the whole species to unremitting terror for that entire time. And this wasn't just an exercise of yahoos up from the city and backwoods beersuckers, this was a ritual joined by teachers, mild-mannered storekeeps, even some mothers and ministers, people who would have raised a fuss about someone kicking a dog or giving a cow the wrong kind of feed, the kind of folks that took their kids to see *Bambi* and wailed their eyes out over *Ol' Yeller.*

Was it mass hysteria? It certainly wasn't for the meat. Was it something rising in the blood, like the geese all gathering and taking to the sky? It certainly wasn't to be close to nature. Was it just mindless tradition—a thing in its season? In a not-quite-defined but terribly depressing way, it seemed to give me an inkling of why we were really in Vietnam.

· 10 ·
TINA AND OUR FIRST SPRING

We got Tina in late April or early May, a two-year-old registered Jersey, the only registered animal we ever had.

Our first country spring was in *mid-renaissance*. Everywhere life was burgeoning! First had come the early-returning flocks of robins and red-winged blackbirds ... the wet-spot swell of singing spring peepers. Then, antediluvian opossums wobbling out of time-warp hibernation; groundhogs popping up on roadsides like chubby heralds; a few disoriented wasps and bees; an explosion of baby bunnies.

Then one day we'd catch the darting glimpse of a red fox. (If it was catlike on its feet, had the gait of a tiny trotter, and was gone before you knew what you saw, it was probably a fox.) And the next day we'd have to slam on our brakes to avoid a pair of oversexed raccoons in reckless heat racing across the road. Even loners like great blue herons and red-tailed hawks were flying in pairs. Here and there: red-belly snake, toad, white-faced hornet, mourning-cloak butterflies followed by red admirals and azure blues. (Mourning cloaks are medium-sized silky black butterflies whose wing edges look like tattered lace embroidered with gold; unlike most butterflies—who live for only one season, whose progeny each spring had to meta-morphose in cocoons—mourning cloaks live for several years, hibernating winters in hollow logs, which allows them to be first out as soon as the weather warmed.)

The streams and culverts were full and rushing, the flora burbling with buds, flowers, intoxicating scents, every tender and succulent shade of green . . . our pear tree a rippling quilt of white flowers, each flower an open nectar purse with a bee's proboscis digging for gold.

On Easter Sunday, Ed Dombroski showed up with hair slicked down, in his best (perhaps only) suit, and asked whether we'd mind if he took a walk in the old woods to look at the flowering dogwoods, and look for a flowering arbutus that—like the dogwoods—had some kind of traditional religious significance for him, and that for many years he'd been going out to take solace from when he got home from early Easter mass. He invited us to join his pilgrimage, but we declined, pretty sure he really wanted to be alone, and he seemed to appreciate our sensitivity to that. He told us where to look for the arbutus and when it was most likely to be in bloom.

In retrospect, the arbutus may not have been as important

to Ed as it had then seemed, or maybe returning to the farm was just too painful for him; whatever the reason, that first spring was the last time he ever came back to look for it. In several different springs, following Ed's instructions, we tried to find the arbutus ourselves, but we never did.

On one of our early-spring walks down the road, we did, however, discover a tiny pond beside the woods that filled only in spring; a large puddle, really, in which frogs and newts and salamanders laid their eggs in various long strands and viscous globs. We fished out one of the jellylike globs, just the right size to fit the palm of a hand, carefully examined the translucent eggs and tiny suspended creatures already taking shape in its primordial goo . . . allowed ourselves to relish its cool slimy shaky wetness for a few moments before gently sliding it back into the shallow pond.

Immediately, I knew that this was *my* arbutus, a feeling that I'd come back for and pay homage to year after year. Unlike the arbutus, though, this was no symbolic grail of innocence meant to put me in mind of some supernatural meaning; rather, in a very down-to-earth way, this quaking jelly awakened feelings and recognitions that reached from my hand and eye and mind . . . back through chromosomal time, my own mortality and prebirth . . . to the first moment that life began, protected and fed by nothing more than its own glob of trembling jelly.

So transcendent and inclusive was this feeling that I felt quite sure, regardless of philosophically different underpinnings, that our feelings and Ed's were probably not very different; our two spring rituals producing similarly visceral chills of humility and awe, regardless of provenance.

As overwhelmed as we were by spring's abundance (burgeoning also in our basement, attic, even our walls), we still felt something was missing. Ahog's absence had left a hole. Not that we had second thoughts about slaughtering him, but we were missing the routine and responsibility; we also thought it important to get another animal quickly so we wouldn't be tempted to sentimentalize Ahog.

And so we got Tina.

· 11 ·

TINA AND MIDNIGHT

Tina was small even for a Jersey, which, as a breed, is about as small as cows get. The reason we got her so cheaply, though, wasn't because of her smallness but because she only had one eye. The other had been lost on a barn nail when she was a calf, a condition that had left her a little skitsy . . . so, rather than butchering her, Ken Gibbs sold her to us at a real good price, probably figuring that having our special attention and a whole barn to herself might even calm her down.

It didn't.

Tina stayed a nervous animal to the end, unexpectedly balking or kicking, once even jumping Bobbie from behind like a bull looking for sex. Seeing a cow draped over Bobbie like that was a ridiculous picture and might've even been funny except for the nasty bruises it left on her thighs and the residual fear that kept Bobbie from ever turning her back on Tina again. Tina may have been small for a cow, but, of course, *smallness* is relative.

After Tina died, I wrote a short story about it, later selling it to *Redbook*, my first sale to a major magazine. In the story I wrote that Tina was "500 pounds or so," and some farm woman from Illinois wrote in that I obviously didn't know the first thing about cows " . . . a 500-pound cow? No wonder she died. Poor thing must've *starved* to death!"

Still, at 500 pounds or so, she had about as much beef in her as any two Green Bay Packers put together, and when she stepped on your foot or leaned into you or suddenly leapt your way, she was plenty big enough to get your attention.

Nor was the woman from Illinois right about our not knowing the first thing about cows. It wasn't like we thought milk came from cartons. There were just more things that we didn't know than things we did. So we asked neighbors, called the vet or Kenneth and Virginia Gibbs, who especially knew about Jerseys, and they answered our questions one at a time and, for the most part, told us we were doing fine.

Despite her high-strung nature, Tina quickly became a great pleasure to us. The old barn was alive again and full of rich, pungent life smells. Every morning and night one of us refilled her water tub and gave her a handful of sweet sorghumy grain, her bony head pushing against arm and wrist while her long purplish tongue curled into the handful of grain to lick it in.

I built a large stall that opened into a back pasture, which I frugally fenced in with some old barbed wire that I'd found still coiled on a slowly rotting hedgerow stump. Unfortunately, finding the weaknesses both of the old materials and my poor fencemanship, Tina quite regularly worked one section or another loose enough for her to climb through. Once out, she usually just stood on the other side of the fence, often pushing her head back through the fence in order to graze the same grass she'd just left. One time, however, she figured out how to go all the way around and get back into the barn on the other side of her stall where we kept the grain in a 20-gallon stainless-steel trash can. Then, nosing the cover off the container, she proceeded to gorge on the grain until she bloated herself almost to death. The vet came out and prescribed two weeks' worth of medicine that needed to be injected down her esophagus through a long plastic tube. Showing us how to do it, Doc McCarthy grabbed hold of her upper lip, pulled it up and back in order to force her head up and mouth open, and then teased the injector tube down her gullet and *zap* !—a piece of cake. For us, however, this was a two-person full-tilt boogie! But we got it done, nursed Tina back to health, moved the grain can into the milkhouse, and I rigged up an electric fence around the pasture that quickly let her know which side of the fence was which.

Just about the same time that we were getting used to Tina, Virginia Gibbs also arranged for us to get some chickens, a dozen Rhode Island Reds for two bucks apiece with a banty rooster thrown in for free. We got the chickens for eggs, just as we had gotten Tina with the intent of milking her. Our experience with Ahog had been an important one, but now we were looking for a different kind of relationship, one that was longer term, in which "nurturing" was not synonymous with "fattening up."

Naturally, before Tina would give milk we had to get her

pregnant, and that left us with the choice of arranging for either a bull or an artificial inseminator. In the balance, we also wondered if we couldn't have her bred to the sperm of a beef-cattle breed. After all, we weren't looking to start a dairy herd; we just wanted enough milk for our own use, a little extra to give away or barter, or maybe try our hand at making cheese or butter. What's more, raising our own beef was certainly every bit as country and practical as raising our own pork. When we looked further into the possibility, we found out that indeed it could be done, as long as we used a breed like Black Angus that typically had small calves. So that's what we did.

For several weeks we tried to determine when Tina was in heat. *Unusual Nervousness* was one of the things we'd been told to look for, but with Tina nervousness was never unusual. A slight redness around the rump was supposedly another clue . . . and a different way of holding her tail. Whatever gave it away, one day Bobbie said it was time. I said I didn't know— I really couldn't see anything different at all.

"A hell of a bull you'd make!" she said. "Just trust me on this, will you?"

It was midsummer when the artificial inseminator came out with his chemistry set full of vials—and astounded us by grabbing hold of Tina's tail and putting the sperm injector so far into her uterus that his arm disappeared all the way up to his shoulder, which caused Tina to bawl in discomfort and surprise. Yet she never kicked or leapt or resisted in any way.

Being pregnant mellowed Tina, I think. I know she got mellower; I'm just not sure if the reason had to do with her getting pregnant or if it was simply that we got mellower with her, firmer and more confident and ultimately more relaxed.

That July I brought in a field of hay by hand . . . using a scythe, pitchfork, and a '61 Chevy pickup that I bought for $400 from a Penn Yan man who'd lost his driver's license on a DWI. Bringing in 15 or 20 loads of mostly timothy and bird's-foot trefoil, I created a story-and-a-half–high haystack in the upper barn that fed Tina through the winter . . . and provided Star with a perfect place for her den later that same winter.

That was also the winter that a ruptured disc in my back turned me into a semi-invalid from early January until I finally gave in to surgery on April Fool's Day. Three weeks after the operation I was back on my feet, and, in gratitude, I finally got around to building a large covered porch beside the house. (What's a country house without a porch!) The first week that I started on the porch, we had a visit from a longtime friendly acquaintance of mine and her Dutch boyfriend. Because Janice was two years younger than I, I had only known her vaguely when we were both in South Bend. I'd gotten to know her better when we were both at Michigan. Now she and Vim were living together in Manhattan, stopping for a rest over at our place on their way back to South Bend . . . where Vim was going to be meeting her parents for the first time.

I had just poured cement that day for the foundation footing for the new porch. And it was that night that Tina gave birth. We knew she was ready and for the past week or so we'd been checking her every night. This night it was Bobbie's turn, and sometime around midnight she suddenly shook me awake and told me it was happening. By the time I got to the barn—amidst the pungent and heady smell of hay and manure and still-steaming afterbirth—I saw a beautiful pitch-black calf sprawled beside Tina, its glossy eyes looking exactly like star sapphires. We named it Midnight. From our readings and conversations, we knew that it was important to get the newborn on its feet and sucking as soon as possible.

We got Midnight on his feet without too much trouble, but Tina wasn't having any of it. Twice when we tried to bring Midnight to her, she kicked him away, the second time hitting him so squarely we were afraid she might even kill him. It was colostrum that the calf needed, the mother's first milk that was rich in protein and antibodies. When we approached Tina to see if she'd let us milk some of the colostrum out of her, she kicked us away, too, catching Bobbie solidly on one hand.

We were getting panicky. I was also a little angry. While Bobbie ran back to the house to call our neighbor Frank, I tried yelling at Tina: "Come on, Tina, *goddamn it* , be a mother—that's enough of this shit!" When she kicked me away from her again, I got some rope and shackled her back legs so she couldn't kick. Then, after petting her, trying to gentle her for a few minutes, I got down under her and carefully caressed her fleshy pink teats. Bobbie returned just in time to see me squeeze out the first colorless, sweet-smelling spurt. By the time Frank arrived, we were both sticky wet with colostrum, and the bucket was half-full. Frank just about fell down laughing at the sight of us on our hands and knees squirting cow juice, but he had to admit that we were getting it done. Midnight's bluish tongue licked the sticky sweetness from our fingers, and we led his muzzle into the bucket. After Midnight had taken all the colostrum he wanted, Frank helped us make him a bed of hay close—but not too close—to Tina.

"It's not too unusual, especially on the first calf," he said. "I'm sure she'll accept him in the morning. You did a great job, don't worry. Try and get some sleep. That's what I'm gonna do. Thanks for callin' me, though."

I unbound Tina, making sure that Midnight was well out of her reach; and Bobbie and I went back to bed—stealing back into the house like teenage lovers—making quiet love, trying not to wake our guests—dozing off a few times, but too excited to really sleep. As soon as the banty rooster started crowing, we got dressed quickly, woke Zack and took him to see the new calf. When we got to the barn the calf looked eager and fine, but Tina was dead. She lay on her side, her belly more distended than when the calf had still been in her, her legs sticking straight out like an overturned kitchen table, her eyes the same cloudy blue sapphire as Midnight's but minus the stars, minus any sign of life at all. One look and whiff left no doubt; left only this carcass of former life, this stiff, bloated carcass now smelling of sour milk and death.

Zack's cherry lips and huge brown eyes opened wide, enthralled by the bawling, wobbly, purple-tongued calf. But then suddenly his attention turned to ours and followed our dewy, pinched stares to Tina.

"What's wrong with Tina?" he asked.

"Tina's dead."

"Why is Tina dead?"

"We don't know."

"But why does she look like that?"

"That's what being dead looks like."

"But why is Tina dead?"

"We don't know, she just is. We'll call Doc McCarthy—maybe he'll know why. Come on, let's go call him," Bobbie said.

Doc McCarthy surmised that she died of a prolapsed uterus, that there was probably nothing we could have done even if we had known.

"Was the calf too big?"

"I don't think so; it just happens sometimes."

He told us where we could get some colostrum from a big Holstein farm out past Old Bath Road and told us whom we should call to dispose of Tina. About ten o'clock the renderer arrived and I fought back tears . . . from lack of sleep . . . from thinking that she'd been dying all that time . . . and from the incredible waste of it. I wanted to make some use of her. I wished we could have butchered her, at least, but she was already bloated, and the possibility of that was long past. Instead, while Bobbie kept Zack away in the house, I watched them winch her up into the old truck next to the carcass of an old skin-and-bones horse that looked like it had been starved to death. Then I paid the men $35, and off they went.

When I got back to the house, our guests were finally up.

"God, you sure get up early! Did we miss anything?" Janice asked.

"Yes, our calf was born last night, but the mother died."

"Really? My God, I'm sorry. Jesus, you're really *doing* it, aren't you? Wow! I still think of you living in the dorm. It's so hard to believe you really live on a farm!"

· 12 ·

MIDNIGHT AND LINDA SKINK

In his first few formative months, Midnight knew no one but us. He had no mother to nurture him, no siblings to compete with, no herd to follow, in fact no example of cowdom at all save for those original few hours with dying Tina, who wanted nothing to do with him. Nonetheless, Midnight was perfectly bovine, untraumatized, essentially an amiably placid, dim-witted grazer who would occasionally get it into his cramped, bony skull that it was a good time to ramble.

Those were very heady days for us. Zack was emerging from the obstinate twos and was well into the sweetly curious almost-threes. My back was nearly normal again, and Bobbie was pregnant again. I sold my *Tina* story to *Redbook.* And the farm was glorious. We planted a huge garden and had a pond dug. Every morning we fed the chickens and looked for eggs, usually collecting two or three or four, each seeming like the rarest of pearls, large, opalescent, still warm. There was some-thing about finding an egg that had to make you smile. And Midnight was another kind of pleasure; after bottle-feeding him for several weeks, we gradually weaned him out into the pasture behind the barn. He didn't seem unhappy, not even when the vet neutered him with a tight rubber band. Still, deciding that he ought to have some kind of bovine compan-ionship, in the late summer we got a six-month-old Holstein heifer that Zack named Linda Skink.

Our daughter Annie was born that fall, leaving us with little extra energy for cows. Feeding and watering them through the winter had become more of a chore than anything else, as it had with the old chickens whose egg production had petered out to nil by the time the snow flew.

By the next spring, Linda and Midnight had reached about two-thirds of their adult size and had also developed a kind of adolescent friskiness. One day Linda caught me unawares and *bit* me on the hand. It was not a serious wound, but she managed to slice my two middle knuckles down to the bone. While I doubted that the spot had enough meat to stitch, I thought I at least ought to have it looked at and went down to see old Doc R—— in Dundee, who saw patients in the downstairs of his house, the waiting room and examination room separated only by a drawn curtain and an open door. This was a fairly common setup, and it was not at all unusual for one of the old docs to be treating a patient at the same time that he was participating in a conversation in the waiting room, which made it feel like something between a veterinary clinic and a barbershop.

Frankly, I had never heard of a cow biting anyone before, and neither had the doc.

"COW BITE?—" Doc yowled, then yelled to everyone in the waiting room, "GUY HERE SAYS HE'S BIT BY A COW! ANY YOU FOLKS EVER HEAR OF A BITIN' COW?"

A lot of laughter followed, mixed in with a few weak attempts at bantering wit. "DON'T WANNA TELL YOU IT WAS REALLY HIS WIFE!"

"HEY, DOC—MAYBE YOU BEST GIT A PICTURE FOR THE MEDICAL BOOKS!" That kind of stuff. I didn't find it all that funny. Just because I hadn't stuck my hand in a corn picker or a bush hog . . . Well, maybe it was *kind* of funny. As it turned out, Doc R—— didn't even charge me.

"Can't let word out that I'm chargin' folks for fixin' cow bites," he said, loud enough for his magnanimity to be overheard.

Linda Skink's biting the hand that fed her was certainly an anomaly, and also nicely symbolic of our bovine buddies' adolescent friskiness, the main expression of which was their ramblin' ways. At that time I had their pasture surrounded by an electric fence, the problem being that Midnight was short and stocky while Linda Skink was long-legged and a jumper. Once she realized that she could jump over the fence, there was no keeping her in until I raised the fence, which was a full day's job. The next morning, Midnight was gone—with the fence raised, he'd managed to slip under it. Another day shot again moving the electric wire, but *this* time, after splitting the difference between the two heights, I came in and told Bobbie I was pretty sure I'd gotten it just right.

The next morning, they were both gone. Not only gone, but we couldn't find them . . . and much of the next three days we spent walking fields, driving roads, calling neighbors to see if anyone had seen two wayward cows. On the fourth day, a farmer called the radio to say he had two cows in his buckwheat field and the owner better come round 'em up—before they ate themselves to death or he turned them into hamburger. The farmer's buckwheat field turned out to be about three miles from us, and I spent most of another day walking them home, driving them cross-country with a stick through overgrown fields, steering them away from crop fields, feeling almost pioneerlike—which was not a bad one-time feeling . . . but I'd also lost a whole week's writing time to these dumb beasts, and, by the time I got them home, I didn't know anymore why we had them. We'd originally intended to raise Linda Skink to milk her, but that now seemed more bother than it was worth. Cows needed to be milked every day. If we left town for a few days, we couldn't very well ask friends or neighbors to milk our cow for us while we were on vacation.

Before summer was out, we sold Linda Skink to a big dairy farm down past Lakemont. We kept Midnight through the summer and fall—waited until Zack was with Bobbie's parents in Detroit for a week—and then called Ray Trojanowski who came out with his rifle and his *litterchure* and asked if I was yet ready to step into the light.

This time we decided to do the butchering ourselves. While Zack was still away, we bought a meat saw and got a pamphlet from Cornell Extension called "Let's Cut Meat." It was surprisingly difficult and gave us a real appreciation of the work butchers did. Although, after much sawing, analyzing and careful cutting, I triumphantly held up a piece of cow that was unmistakably a rump roast! By the time our kitchen table was heaped with roasts that actually looked like roasts and steaks that actually looked like steaks, we were giddy from the accomplishment of it.

This time, though—unlike with Ahog—we left *The Foxfire Book* on the shelf and did not try to make soap or candles or try any recipes with brains, hooves or tail.

· 13 ·

MR. THIS AND MR. THAT

The whole "Mr. ——" business started with Mr. Toad, when Zack was two or three. We had a large toad living in the crawl space under our front porch—from Zack's knee-high viewpoint a creature whose wartiness, bulging eyes and sudden jumps engendered curiosity and also uncertainty.

"It's only a toad, he can't hurt you. Here, you can touch him—very, very gently. Okay, let's let him go. Mr. Toad lives here with us. He lives under the porch."

Something like that. And then whenever we saw him again, "Oh look, it's Mr. Toad!" In that diminutive, slightly dim-witted way in which parents introduce their little ones to the world.

Pretty soon there were "misters" all over the place: Mr. Turtle. Mr. Groundhog. Mr. Rabbit. Mr. This and Mr. That. It wasn't anything we consciously did, just a Disneyesque way of trying to make the natural world seem a bit more personal and friendly.

But, of course, often nature is not personal. And sometimes when it's personal, it's not the least bit friendly. There's the Disney way. And there's also the way of the Brothers Grimm.

Under the deck in back of the house lived Mr. Snake—a very large garter snake (who also probably spent a good deal of his time in our basement).

"Oh look, Zacky—there's Mr. Snake. Yes, you can touch him, very gently though."

Then one day while Zack was romping around the

backyard, just under the deck he came upon Mr. Snake . . . with half of Mr. Toad sticking out of his mouth. Uncomfortably, I tried to explain that that's how Mr. Snake lived . . . by eating mice and toads. He had Mr. Toad—who was struggling desperately but inexorably losing ground—by his two back legs, wart by wart vacuuming him in.

For Zack's sake—although it was normally against my principles—I interfered and freed the toad from the snake's jaws. In my cupped hands, I brought Mr. Toad's still-slimy rear end back around to the front of the house; but before I let him hop back under the porch, I told him—with Zack listening— that this was a one-time-only reprieve.

" . . . and if you're a smart Mr. Toad, you'll *stay* on this side of the house!"

· 14 ·
PLAYING GOD (THE GARDEN)

In our first spring we also planted a garden. Like gods with perfect *chutzpah*, we just pointed at a convenient spot in the wild fields behind the house and said: *There* —THAT will be our *garden!* Frank came over with his Farmall tractor and plowed the spot exactly the way we wanted it, laying open the earth as if he were cutting out a center square of divinity fudge. At one point, after the perimeter had been established, he let me try my hand and showed me how to work the power take-off and three-point hitch, and suddenly there I was, watching back over my shoulder as the earth transformed to garden at the touch of my hand.

Frank's rule of thumb was that—except for a few early things like onions, lettuce, and peas—the garden shouldn't be planted until Memorial Day; then you could be pretty sure you wouldn't get a killing frost after that. Most years, though, we couldn't stand waiting that long and got most of our garden in as soon as April and May started begging for it. We also figured that with the shortness of Yates County summers and our poor soil quality, it needed all the summer it could get. A few times Frank proved right, and a late frost forced us to replant; but that still seemed better than waiting around through most of the spring with nothing in the ground.

That first year we planted everything: carrots, onions, radishes, two kinds of tomatoes, three kinds of peas, four kinds of beans, five kinds of squash, six kinds of greens, seven different herbs, eight rows of early corn, eight rows of late. Also cukes and zukes, bell and banana peppers (hot and not), cauliflower, broccoli, brussels sprouts, muskmelons, water-melons, eggplants—even peanuts, Jerusalem artichokes and oyster root! And in the four corners, looking clockwise from the house, rhubarb, pumpkins, asparagus, and grapes . . . with morning glories, gourds and sunflowers on the side fences and marigolds, zinnias, gladiolas and cosmos between the rows.

Lesson 1. Because the garden had far exceeded our needs—not to mention our energy and dedication—the next spring we brought in the fence and reduced it by about 25 percent. And the following year by 25 more.

Lesson 2. *What ye sow so shall ye reap* . . . sort of. Ye shall also reap a myriad of *un*sown—bugs, slugs, voles, moles, beetles, weevils, cutworms, borers, locusts, and larval everything. Not to mention unbelievable yields of prolific weeds and grasses— all competing intensely to survive and dominate the freshly turned square of suddenly available land.

Of course, if the gods had only wanted goodness, they would have just created heaven and left it at that. And if all we had cared about had been perfect flowers and veggies, we would have built a greenhouse. But the greater pleasure must come from creating sustenance and beauty out of *im*perfection —else what's an earth for?

On the other hand, because we never used herbicides or pesticides, our garden was always a riot of struggle and competition—thousands of species and millions of individual organisms vying for space and sustenance; we gardeners trying our best to nurture some and eliminate others—to maximize the chances for our favorites to grow, flourish and bear fruit.

I suppose that this partly-designed/partly-wild condition even generated some of the dynamism and challenge. Not that we liked the idea of sharing with the critters, but it was certainly more palatable than pouring toxic chemicals on our garden year after year. And if some of the corn got blight, if slugs got a few tomatoes, if groundhogs got a squash or two— it was all perfectly natural—and we still usually ended up with more than we could eat, freeze and give away. Even if certain crops failed completely, there was always next year—a little more lime, a little less ash, fix the fence and hope for better weather. It was all gone with the first frost anyway—and, by spring, hope was bound to be renewed.

That was the theory, anyway. In reality, we never managed to be quite so sanguine. When flea beetles rendered healthy eggplant leaves into antique lace; when encroaching quackgrass choked the roots of everything planted within two feet of the fence; when a healthy zuke plant suddenly keeled over because some fat little borer had shredded the pith of its stem, it wasn't *really* a matter of "a little for them, a little for us," but rather *How can we best eliminate them?*

The battle wasn't only against the various weeds, pests and parasites, it was also with our resolve to keep the garden purely natural. When companion planting didn't work, when wood ash didn't keep the flea beetles away, when only a few of the slugs drowned themselves in the pie plates of stale beer, when the quackgrass rhizomes found their way in under the stone-covered black plastic, when we couldn't stand to squish any more of this little bug or that—it took every drop of resoluteness not to go for the big guns, bring in the toxic artillery and just *bomb* the bastards! While certain gardening columns tried to tell us that the meditative process of gardening was even more important than the harvest, our guts knew it was a crock. In a world of so much futility and uncertainty, the garden was supposed to be an island of sanity and order. A source of aesthetic pride. Living proof that careful planning, love, nurturing and hard work rewarded one in direct proportion.

Reaping what you sowed was the whole point.

For as long as Star was around, the deer and rabbits and groundhogs kept their distance. As she was not allowed in the garden herself, she guarded its perimeter jealously. Later though, after Star, we had yearly bouts with rabbits and groundhogs. If weeds and bugs eroded the garden piecemeal through a multitude of nibbles, these larger pests hit it like an avalanche. In one night, a single bunny could take out a whole row of sprouting beans or peas. Groundhogs usually wreaked their havoc later, eschewing sprouts and tender leaves in preference for the fruits themselves; they were particularly fond of almost-ripe pumpkins and squash. As bad as it was to lose a pumpkin that one had been nurturing all summer just as it was finally beginning to turn orange . . . an acorn squash hardly a week from peak pickable ripeness . . . even *worse*, groundhogs loved a good smorgasbord! Not satisfied to just take one whole squash or pumpkin, it often took several bites from a dozen, wiping out half a patch in a single night!

In response: we tried scarecrows, which never worked; bloodmeal, which worked but was expensive and washed away with the first good rain; tying human and dog hair to the fence, which was more work than it was worth; obsessive repairing and rebuilding the fence, which was effective—except that we usually didn't know where the fence needed fixing until after an animal had already gotten in.

I also owned two guns—a .22 given to me by a retired army colonel when I helped him move, and a beautifully worked old shotgun that I bought for $15 at a yard sale. However, we had lived on the farm for seventeen years before I bought any ammunition. For all the enmity we felt at times toward these various invaders, for almost two decades we managed to harvest plenty without ever resorting to herbicides, pesticides or weapons.

· 15 ·

POTATO BEETLES
AND SPITTLEBUGS

It mystifies me that we never saw a potato beetle until we planted potatoes. Where did it come from? What incredible sense apparatus did it have that led it to a tiny potato patch at least half a mile from where any potatoes had grown in at least ten years?

I'm sure that if we'd done some serious potato-bug research, we could have found out why this was. Given, though, that our friends and neighbors and several insect books offered no explanations, we contented ourselves to remain mystified. While part of us might have cringed at the anti-intellectuality of that—we certainly didn't think that taking a bite of knowledge might force us out of the garden, nor did we see the garden as a classroom or laboratory or something that needed to be mastered. We learned a little more each season and enjoyed each bit of knowledge as it came, even about insects.

Potato bugs notwithstanding—for instance, we came to observe a number of garden insects in the surrounding fields. Spittlebugs, for example. Spittlebugs are so named because the tiny yellow-dot nymphs are usually found in a center of sudsy secretion that looks like a small gob of spit. We probably never would've noticed spittlebugs at all except for their love of pea vines. For a long time we couldn't understand it when we found some of the slender stems of our pea vines eaten clean through, their severed tops left withering on the ground. What kind of animal would chomp the stem while eschewing the tender leaves and tops? Some larvae and borers burrow into thick stems, but not into thready vines.

Eventually we began to notice that each of the decapitated pea plants had a gob of white suds near the point of dismemberment; and, upon closer examination, we discovered a pinhead-yellow-speck insect within each gob. Once having identified these culprits as spittlebug nymphs, we daily inspected our pea vines for early signs of drool, from which we could pick out the offenders easily and squash them.

Ironically, the reason that spittlebugs covered themselves in this self-made froth was that it enabled them to hide from predators; however, in our case, it was that very "protective" froth that gave them away.

I had never even seen a spittlebug before finding them on our peas; consequently, I concluded that they were a parasite specific to peas in the way of potato bugs and asparagus beetles. But then I began to see the telltale spit gobs on several other kinds of plants outside the garden—on thistles and clover, for example—and I realized that they had been living around me all my life, I just hadn't noticed them until we planted peas.

From the spittlebugs I also realized that the garden was not so much an attractor of bugs as it was an attractor of our attention to them. The garden was where we were on our hands and knees digging in the soil, examining each plant like properly protective parents, and this centered our curiosity and led us to pay closer attention to insect specifics so that we could better distinguish friend from foe. In our front yard I might not have bothered noticing the differences between ladybugs and spotted cucumber beetles; but in the garden ladybugs fed on destructive aphids, while cucumber beetles fed on all our cruciferous vegetables. The garden prompted us to learn that scary-looking earwigs helped to break down old wood and stalks, that praying mantises devoured locusts as well as their mates, that there were as many beneficial beetles in the garden as destructive ones.

Generally, it became our rule that if we didn't know what a bug was and didn't actually see it eating a plant, we left it alone—with the exception of larvae. We always tossed them out, figuring that if they were beneficial, they could come back as adults, when we could better tell what they were.

· 16 ·

INSECTS ON PARADE

In addition to the garden's being an attractor of certain creatures and an attractor of our attention to them, there were a few species that came to the garden because they were attracted to *us*. This category belonged almost exclusively to biting flies. I don't think they really *knew* the garden as a special place and waited for us there. Rather, I think the scenario played itself over and over again in just the same way. While we were happily working away in one place, one or two of them happened upon our sweaty scent and then somehow rang the dinner bell for their compatriots, and we were suddenly inundated.

Our biting flies came in three waves: blackflies in early

June; no-see-ums in mid- to late June; deerflies and horseflies in July and August.

Blackflies, the gnat-size little devils, came in hordes . . . earlobes, eyelids and scalps being their most delectable pièces de résistance.

No-see-ums, so called because of their pinpoint size, usually came out while the blackflies were still there and stayed for about a month. Despite the silliness of their name, a swarm of no-see-ums could also send you back to the house in short order. While their bites were not really painful, there was something psychologically unnerving about frequent pinprick attacks coming from something you couldn't see or hear.

In direct contrast to no-see-ums, with deerflies and horseflies it was exactly their size and noise, their continuous flitting and buzzing that was so unsettling, especially since their bites were also considerably more painful; as soon as the buzzing lessened, one began to imagine them poised to bite on every rolling sweatdrop. The swept-wing deerflies were a special nuisance. Fortunately, the bumblebee-sized horseflies —whose bites often drew blood and left strawberry welts— were fewer and more cautious about landing on humans, much preferring animals of barn and pasture.

Something there is that doesn't love an insect, I suppose. And yet, despite the fact that some of them sting, bite, spread disease, ruin crops, invade (even eat) our homes, I think our dislove for them has more to do with their smallness, the fact that we don't see them very well, which makes them seem *sneaky*. They move in and out of places where we can't see them.

They leap, they crawl, they come through the air, they swim, they burrow, they look like rocks and twigs and leaves—suddenly they're just there. *Them!* Not only are they too small for us to take them seriously as individuals, but they're also almost impossible to look in the eye. Looking something in the eye is the way that we judge its character and intent, the content of its soul. But only under magnification can we look an insect in the eye, and then—*egad!*—what comes back at us is the alien stuff of nightmares! Eyes that look everywhere at once but never meet ours. What kind of hellish nonsouls do these windows look into?

And not only are they sneaky, small and impossible to individualize, but they come in hatches, hordes and hives, in too many varieties even for us to catalog effectively.

What's more, because of their smallness, survival has required them to become outfitted with an enormous array of protective devices: gorgon faces, unsquashable armors, weapons both real and faux, camouflages so exact that some look like leaves and twigs right up to the nodes, veins and drops of dew. Thus, we can never be quite sure when they're with us and when they aren't, what we're dealing with and what we aren't.

And yet . . . one can get into a mood to admire insects: their antiquity, their magnificent adaptability, their ability to carry life's message in so many guises. They may seem alien and mechanical, putting no value in the "one" except as a vassal of the "many," but there's another way to look at it. Because so few insect offspring ever live to reproduce, nature places great value on the mutant insect, the extraordinary individual who jumps a little higher, flies a little faster, hides a little better, demonstrates or bluffs a greater repugnance or ferocity. Any change that increases the chance of survival is more likely to be reproduced, and it's because insects reproduce so often and in such great numbers that there are so many insect species with so many diverse abilities; billions of tiny changes continually maximize insect chances to be the right individual in the right place and time to survive and reproduce. Insects have been Evolution's darlings for a billion years expressly because of the importance of "individual" changes. This may even be seen as Evolution's way of ensuring that the weak inherit the earth.

In fact, we certainly need insects much more than they need us. They have carried life's banner almost from the beginning into the present and continue to be a great part of the natural balance that sustains us.

Even aesthetically we would miss them greatly. Not only because they pollinate flowers, make honey, and are food for fish and birds—we would miss them in their own right. Biting flies and mosquitoes may come in waves and hatches, but so do june bugs, lightning bugs, dragonflies, butterflies, and August's culminating euphonic pulse of crickets, katydids and mantises that has left its imprint in us . . . one of the haunting soul-filling places where music comes from.

· 17 ·

PLAYING GOD (THE POND)

Digging the pond cost us $847.32 and was the best money we ever spent. About 80 yards to the side of the barn and 100 yards behind the house, there was a long, gentle downslope that leveled off to a marshy cattailed spot that just seemed to call out for a pond. I had the Yates County Water & Conservation man come out. Back then there was still some 50/50 state money to help pay for the engineering and development of approved pond sites. The agent agreed that the wet spot and the lay of the land held promise, but said we'd need to have some test holes dug so he could make a proper geological assessment.

Having no idea who to call to get a test hole dug, I asked Frank, who told me that Peewee down in Dundee was real good—if you could get him. The thing about Peewee was that he never kept much a schedule, so whoever woke him up earliest was most likely to get him for the day. About 6:30 the next morning, I found his edge-of-town house that had a backhoe in the yard and knocked until Peewee staggered blearily to the door. When he stopped grumbling long enough to take a breath, I told him I'd buy him breakfast down at Ken's Luncheonette. After breakfast, he hauled his backhoe up to our place and dug four deep test holes. The conservation agent met us there and, after examining the holes, determined that while two of the spots looked possible, there was too much shale too close to the surface, which could easily keep the pond from holding, for him to officially approve any of the sites.

When the agent had gone, Peewee said it was a bunch of bull and if we wanted a pond we should dig it anyway—never mind any damn approval. He didn't have enough equipment to do it himself, but suggested Charlie Hill.

After examining the test holes, Charlie Hill was not as optimistic as Peewee had been, but said we had a lot of clay in our soil that he could pack down over the shale, and while he wouldn't give us any kind of guarantee, he thought it would probably hold. With some hesitancy, we agreed that he should go ahead. A few weeks later, he returned with a backhoe, two dump trucks and a big dozer, and in less than three days shaped the spot into what looked like a giant clamshell: closed and shallow at the front, gradually splaying out on two curving sides, the hollowed middle rising to meet the graceful dike that spread like a fan around the back. At the lowest point, he left a runoff spot so that the water wouldn't ever wash over and erode the top of the dike.

The entire basin covered about half an acre; its deepest point was about nine feet below the top of the dike. After packing the bottom with clay, on our instructions, Charlie shallowed the sides to less than a foot, to minimize the chance of a child ever falling in over its head.

Then he wrote us up a bill for $847.32.

At the time it seemed like a lot of money, especially since all we had to show for it was this scraped raw piece of our land. And if the conservation agent's fear proved right and the pond didn't hold, this huge ugly crater would not only remain as a reminder of money down the hole, but also as a monument to our hubris—mockingly visible from house, garden, barn and pasture.

That winter, though—covered with fresh snow—the dug basin turned exquisite as frosted Steuben glass. In the spring, the melted snow half-filled the pond, and the grass seed that we'd spread began to sprout on the sides and dike along with wild seeds from the fields—mostly timothy, clover and bird's-foot trefoil—which also began to heal its rawness.

With the spring rains, several small springs came alive in the bottom of the pond. The water rose quickly to within two or three feet of the dike's top. Gradually, the silty water began to settle and clear and, as soon as the weather began to warm, spring peepers gave the pond its first voice. A few weeks later, bullfrogs began ga-*LUNG*-ing. And then a great blue heron dropped in.

In midsummer, I caught some fish from Frank's pond to stock ours: five small largemouth bass and just one sunfish—for good luck, I guess. The sunfish had badly overcrowded the bass in Frank's pond, and we didn't want that to happen in ours.

By then the water had cleared completely, the grass had taken hold, and the pond had become a lush, sparkling wonder of new life and seclusion. Because of the way it hunkered down, unseeable except from our own land, it was ideal for solitude and skinny-dipping. In July and August, after a hot day's work on the house or garden, or pitching hay or manure in or out of the barn, nothing was sweeter than throwing off sweaty clothes and diving into the cold, clear water of the pond.

· 18 ·
MATING NEWTS

The next winter, we skated on the pond. With spring, after the peepers had broken the ice, I started circling the pond day after day looking for the fish, hoping they'd survived the winter. I saw three different kinds of frogs and a painted turtle. Where'd *they* come from? I saw an early groundhog sunning on the dike. One morning I scared up a doe and two spotted fawns. But no sign of the fish.

It wasn't until the temperature got up around 80 and stayed there for a few days that the fish suddenly showed in the shallows, all five bass and the sunfish. All looked perfectly at home, rising occasionally to feed at the surface. (Numerous aquatic insect species had also found their way to the pond.) Although I didn't realize it at the time, the female bass weren't so much feeding as aggressively defending the territory around their nests, which they'd built in the shallows for the necessary plant cover. Insects, amphibians and reptiles competed for the same protection, and a month later the pond shallows were swarming with various tadpoles, naiads and minnow-size bass fry.

Before that, though, before the reappearance of the fish, even before the three days and nights of incessant frog serenading and frantic copulation, one day I happened onto a scene that I'd never seen before and I've never seen since. In the very shallowest part of the pond, in perhaps two or three inches of water, I spotted an amazingly beautiful red-spotted orange newt swimming among the feathery tendrils of some tenuous aquatic plants. The water was perfectly clear and the newt's graceful swimming seemed almost like a dance. I hunkered down, entranced. A foot or so beyond, in slightly deeper water, I saw a second newt. As it came in toward the first, a third newt suddenly rushed up to divert it. Those two circled each other, occasionally lunging and countering at each other, though mostly undulating in place and whipping their tails wildly.

Then I saw a third male; and, while all three of them postured and battled, the female kept sliding gracefully from side to side, in and out of the ferny grottos of her underwater nest, her own gently swishing tail feathered with some kind of ruffled keel. Now and then one of the males left the other two and tried to approach the nest, but each time the female chased him back. I watched this for something like an hour before she finally relented, came out and led one of the males back to her mating chamber. I couldn't figure out how the victor was chosen; whether it was something that the males had settled first among themselves, or whether she had finally found something to prefer in one over the others. All of this in no more than three fingers of water in a clump of delicate weeds no bigger than a saucer. I was so enamored by them that when the male and female finally got to coupling, I thanked them silently for the performance and left discreetly. I later read that in the wild whipping of their tails the males exuded an intoxicating scent that in some way influenced the female's choice.

I don't exactly know why I never saw newts mating again. For one thing, the water was rarely as translucent as on that particular day; for another, the layering of aquatic plants was never again so sparse and light; but I think the main reason was that in later years the proliferation of bass marauding the perimeter shallows simply prevented the newts from being able to enjoy such leisurely courting.

· 19 ·

THE LURE OF THE POND

The second summer I built a small screenhouse from some odds and ends of lumber and old window screens, a primitive airy structure nestled almost to the water's edge, really more of a glorified playpen than anything else. By then Annie was nine months old and trying to toddle; the screenhouse was intended as a place for her to play or nap while we spent time with Zack or managed a few pond moments for ourselves, but it never worked out that way because even then Annie was two-fisted about such things and not about to stay quietly put as long as she could see us unrestrained and cavorting out in the great wide world. Some children are content to be within sight of the action; Annie always wanted to be at the heart of it.

As a result, the screenhouse was almost never used; by the next summer Annie was splashing around in the pond, Zack was at the "Watch me! Watch me!" stage, and the pond certainly didn't need any auxiliary structures other than the ten-foot plank dock that stepped one over the muck and weeds at the pond's edge, so—less than a year after building it —I tore it down, returning the screen and lumber to the barn.

Lesson One at the pond was that children were not allowed to ever be at the pond without supervision until they could swim from the makeshift dock to the dike and back again without touching bottom. Zack was nearly nine before he passed the "Pond Test." Annie, forever trying to catch up to her big brother, doggedly paddled her way across and back the very next summer, when she was still only six.

With fishing, too—Annie was not only baiting worms and taking fish off the hook almost as soon as Zack was, but while he was still squeamish about cleaning his catch, she couldn't wait to get her hands on the knife and scaler, slit the bass open to see which had the male gonads and which held the tight bundles of golden roe.

For observing animals in their natural habitats, we could hardly have had a richer microcosm. There were the seasonal and perennial regulars:

Various frogs—calling, mating, laying eggs, hatching to tadpoles, sprouting legs, some leaving the pond, some staying.

A plethora of aquatic insects: dragonflies, mayflies, damselflies, stone flies, caddis flies, dobsonflies, boatmen, back swimmers and diving beetles.

Numerous birds: sandpipers, plovers, killdeer. For the first few years we had a kingfisher, shrieking its call as it hovered over the water, before suddenly dramatically plunging for a meal. Swirling barn swallows ubiquitously fed on flies and mosquitoes; thrushes, robins and red-winged blackbirds perched near their nests in the cattailed corners. Quite often a great blue heron parachuted down for a meal.

For a few weeks every spring, ducks, usually mallards, flew in for a few hours each day, swimming around and bottoming up to feed on strands of algae—although a couple of times we also had black ducks and buffleheads. Just once did a pair of mallards stay to nest and hatch their ducklings, mama duck leading them in swimming or waddling a single-file line like a child's picture book come to life.

The edges of the pond were always imprinted with chiseled bifurcated deer tracks. Although the deer mostly came at night or in the very early morning, we sometimes saw them—approaching warily in threes and fours, a buck or a big doe standing watch while the others skittishly descended for a drink. A few times from my writing window I saw two or three younger deer abandon caution: playing, splashing and chasing each other—gamboling about for ten or fifteen minutes—until a mature doe finally came down and drove them out.

In several years we saw muskrats gracefully scooting and diving around the pond. Frank said that we ought to trap them out because their burrows would ruin the dike. Fortunately, they never stayed long enough for that to be necessary.

Every year we saw something we hadn't seen before.

Once, for just three days, we had a beaver on the pond.

Just once I saw a flock of wild turkeys on the dike.

On December 5, 1985, I saw five raccoons, two large ones and three smaller, walking the length of the dike as though it were an esplanade—in the process of changing winter digs, I presumed.

Just once we saw a green heron.

Just once we saw a large water snake ribboning through the water. Seeing the snake dampened the pleasure of swimming for a few weeks. I have no idea how he got there or where he went, but that was the only time we ever saw a snake in the pond.

While we often saw painted turtles, we once came upon a huge snapping turtle—about a foot in diameter—looking like some Mesozoic throwback with its primordial drab armor plate, triangular spiked tail, crusty clawed feet and nasty disposition. I didn't know if their finger-and-toe-chomping reputation was exaggeration or fact, but I did know I didn't trust it in *our* swimmin' hole. So, after studying it from all angles, we carefully got it into a box and trucked it over to Mud Lake, a large swamp two roads over.

· 20 ·

HERONS

In the air, great blue herons often reminded me of flying reptiles, pterodactyls or somesuch. Except for the whooping crane, sandhill crane, albatross and California condor, their six-foot wingspan is the largest of any North American bird—making them certainly the largest birds in our neck of the woods. Taking off, they lumbered up flapping like circus tents broken from their moorings. Landing, they swooped down, bottoming their lanky bodies into the wind, frantically gyrating their wings in reverse before finally sticking down on their wobbly stilt legs.

Obviously an early flight model, herons looked almost man-made.

On the ground they were equally awkward: Erector-set legs, coilable necks, overlong beaks nearly too big for their heads to hold, all topped by a few ridiculously jaunty plumes, which, in the way that they lay flat—further accentuating their elongated heads—surely made them the Cyrano of birds! And yet, like Cyrano, there was poetry in their grotesqueness and deadliness in their rapier strikes! Woe be it to fish or frog when the silliness was over and the great blue-gray hunter waded in for the kill! Holding ready pose, its neck and harpoon nose suddenly unleashed—*thrust home!* And then, as if in laughing victory—stretching its head high in the air—the heron sucked the lump of its still-wriggling prey down through its long tube neck into its upright Hoover body.

From the window of my writing room which overlooked our pond, I often saw one of these great birds come to hunt. On rare occasions, two came together and staked out opposite sides; but, for the most part, they were lone hunters, so eye-catching and fascinating that when one was there, my prose usually took a purple turn or stopped altogether.

For many years, the now-famous kinetic sculptor George Rhoads lived just down from our neighbors Frank and Joan Boyce on the same dirt road. George was the most creative person I'd ever known. Whenever we dropped over, he was always painting, sculpting, making masks, fountains, oragimi, or working on early models of the fantastic machines that have since earned him international success. His property bordered on some wooded state land where there was a rookery of great blue herons, which he took us to see. I carried Annie on my back as Bobbie, Zack and I carefully followed George into the deepest part of the woods where we beheld a dozen or so herons in their huge treetop nests, each nest five or six feet across, all together looking like a raised village of primitive thatched huts . . . so close to our home . . . this newfound miraculous wonder—the ground heaped with guano, the air filled with ancient squawking, the treetops aflutter with giant wings!

We were sure we'd be coming back to this place, by ourselves and with certain of our dearest friends; but, a month or so later, before we came back even once, George came over to tell us that someone had shot up the rookery, and now it was nothing but ruined abandoned nests.

For the rest of that year, no more herons came to the pond. The year after, we saw one occasionally. Since then—though I no longer knew where they nested—they came almost as frequently as before.

· 21 ·

PARADISE!

As it reached full maturity, the pond was magnificence in every season, our pièce de résistance. By comparison, every other project had been marred by at least some unsettling or embarrassing aspect. Even the garden had its yearly failures. At its best it was hardly a showpiece; it needed constant tending all summer and regeneration every spring.

But the pond was such perfection that it was difficult not to be smug about it. Circumscribing the pond, I mowed the whole six-foot-wide top of the dike and a fifteen- or eighteen-foot swath along the side nearest the barn. On the third triangular side—where we let the willows and cattails provide natural cover for wildlife—I made only a single-pass footpath. The pond was like a hidden jewel, a secret sanctuary where one could walk barefoot (even nude); take a swim or lie on an innertube; study the pond life or fish for bass; sit in the soft grass to read, meditate or just bliss out . . . a place of solitude, full-moon swims, occasionally even lovemaking, groping and undulating on the soft bottom or in the cold rushing current of the underwater springs.

In the fifth or sixth summer, in several different expeditions, Zack and Annie and I caught five of the original fish: four lunker bass and the lone sunfish—the largest bluegill I've ever seen—round as a flounder and weighing at least a pound. Before that we had always released the big ones; but, noticing that none of the young fish were growing nearly as fast as the originals had, we had decided to reduce the competition and give the younger fish a better chance. For sentimental reasons, however, we left one lunker in the pond—for him only, instituting a release policy should he ever be caught. In the ensuing years, he (or she) was dubbed "Granddad." As it turned out, even with the other large fish gone, the pond was still overpopulated; and while a number of the other fish grew to good eating size, none of them ever approached lunker size.

Over the years, Granddad did get hooked three or four times, each time rushing out of the reeds to swallow a smaller fish that was already on the hook. No one ever had a chance to release him, though, because he always broke the line and disappeared with his bellyful of fish and hook before anyone could get to him.

· 22 ·

TROUBLE IN PARADISE

One day, when the pond was fourteen or fifteen years old, I was pulling cattails, an arduous but necessary job because, by then, the cattails and willows and algae and numerous other aquatic plants had increased slowly to a point of nagging unpleasantness. We no longer felt so godlike in regard to the pond, unless it was in the sense of a god who, at the same time that he had Big-Banged his world into creation, had also created Entropy. Maybe it was the necessary price entailed by life and freedom in the material world: Everything that lives ages and dies. Not only plants and animals, but mountains and planets—perhaps even the universe itself. Certainly ponds. And the more natural freedom we had allowed, the sooner we had hastened the pond's aging and decline.

I no longer thought of the pond in transcendent terms. While I still thought that there was a good chance that, in some form or other, the pond would outlive us, our main concern had become to keep it a place that we still enjoyed for as long as we could. I didn't want to become a slave to maintaining the pond, and yet I wasn't about to surrender it into some glorified wetland, either. And so, more and more, I found myself pulling weeds and cattails, trimming willows, filling groundhog and muskrat holes, digging roots.

Having stretched out a wider and longer pier to overreach the increasingly weedy and mucky shallows, we still enjoyed swimming in the pond—almost as much as before.

On this day, however, something seriously detrimental occurred. After I had finished wading the shallows to pull out this particular patch of cattails, as I was getting ready to dive into the clear center of the pond to rinse myself off, I noticed several small slug-worm-like creatures clinging to my ankles. When I wiped them off, I noticed a very small ribbon of blood streaming from each detachment. Unable to deny what I knew they were, the more significant wound spiked into my psyche.

Were I a god, I don't think I would have created leeches—at least not in paradise.

· 23 ·
A NEW YEAR'S EVENT

Our basement was a habitat all its own. Ed Dombroski told us that the original house on our spot had burned down around the turn of the century. The present house had been hauled in a mile or so, dragged cross-country on skids over snow-covered fields by teams of workhorses which had taken most of two winters before the house had actually been set in place. All that remained of the original house was its basement foundation; but because the "new" house was quite a bit larger, the cellar had been big enough to go under only two-thirds of it. That was why the other third of the house had only a short-block foundation and a crawl space.

All in all, it was a various, cobwebby, subterranean habitat, not a place to take relatives and guests. For instance, Bobbie's mother—who loved our country home—was the type of mother who expected to cook, clean and do laundry when she visited, refusing all our efforts to force her into the role of respected guest. However, on one of her first descents into our basement laundry area, she saw a snake in the act of eating a toad, and that was the last time that she ever went into the cellar. It was such a relief to us that I don't even think we bothered telling her that what she so frantically brought us down the steps to witness was something that we'd never seen there before either. We had occasionally seen garter snakes on the indented ledges above our foundation walls, where the masses of electrical wires provided wonderful snake camou-flage. Twice in twenty years we've had to deal with rats—though we never actually saw a live one, only several squirrel-sized corpses after we'd put poison out. Occasionally, we saw a toad or a mouse hop or scamper for cover, but it wasn't as if the basement was *jumping* with life; we simply knew that there was a certain amount of living that went on down there when we weren't looking.

But sometimes one did get the sense of being watched by little eyes.

One New Year's Eve, when the kids were too small to stay up, Bobbie and I broke out some shrimp dip and champagne, content to watch the New Year come in on TV, count it down like an old fighter going out on his back, an Explorer rocket heading into the Great Unknown. A few minutes before twelve, we heard a loud crash in the basement, which I investigated disgruntledly . . . not really expecting anything more than the wind to be moving around down there in midwinter. Having found nothing but the usual dank, creepy silence, I was rushing back up to see the ball drop in Times Square when I almost stepped on a *salamander* halfway up the basement steps! I stopped, then slowly knelt down for a better look...half-expecting it to only be an optical illusion ...especially because of how well it blended with the worn, stained remnant of Oriental rug that we'd tacked down on the cellar stairs, in a vain attempt to civilize our foreboding underworld descent. But it did not melt away before my eyes. Nor did it make any move to escape my overhanging gargoyle-eyed amazement. It was, in fact, a salamander—lizardlike except that its skin was not dry and scaly like a lizard's, but soft and moist, gleaming with a bright colorful pattern that could have passed for leftover Christmas gift-wrapping...deep plum sprinkled with red specks and ringed yellow spots...a beautiful little creature, about six inches long including the three inches of its tail. (A red-spotted salamander, *Ambystoma maculatum*, we later discovered when we looked it up in our *Larousse*.)

What was so startling was not only that we'd never seen one like it, nor any other kind of salamander anywhere in our house or basement, but that we should find it *now*, halfway up our cellar steps, in midwinter, when it should have been sleeping in the mud somewhere, on the very cusp of the New Year!

What's more, it held up its head, its wide, dark eyes looking straight into mine, even when I cupped it gently in my hands and delivered it like a personal New Year's gift under Bobbie's equally astonished gaze.

It was one of those things that made me feel we were being played with, as if had to *mean* something—but we certainly weren't about to give in to that!

Discussing what we should do with it, we were tempted to put it in a makeshift aquarium for a while, but instead we took it back into the basement and let it go, in the sunken always-wet area near the tile drainpipe, where we figured it had probably come in.

By the time we got back to the "occasion" at hand, it was already ten after twelve, ten minutes into the New Year. Even as we kissed and drank a toast to good portents in the New Year, there was a little chill of strangeness that continued to tease us.

· 24 ·

MASON

A second basement oddity had to do with our old cat Jason.

Jason, who'd always been neurotic and reclusive, even in Ann Arbor, finally became senile and incontinent as well. By our third year on the farm, when she was not only urinating regularly on the large potted jade plant and the already-scrawny rubber tree, but had also begun urinating on our bed, Bobbie decided to take her to the vet and have her put down. As Jason had always been more her pet than mine, Bobbie matter-of-factly took the unpleasant responsibility on herself.

I'd gone to New York for a few days, to be with a friend whose play was about to open. When I came back, Jason was gone. I was surprised, and maybe slightly stung that Bobbie hadn't waited for me to return home. Even if I'd never had a great affection for Jason, she had always been with us.

"You were gone. She started peeing on the bed, it was just time. I thought you'd be glad it was over."

"Well, in a way I guess I am."

"It wasn't easy, you know. I had her for a lot of years."

"I know you did. I guess that's why I'm surprised you took it all on yourself."

"It was time," Bobbie said, tears rushing to her eyes.

I gave her a hug. "To Jason," I said, lifting an imaginary glass.

She smiled bravely and raised her empty hand: "To life . . . L'chayim!"

The basement oddity with Jason had occurred a year or so earlier, on a morning in which I was writing and doing laundry at the same time. When my imagination went blank or I was butchering some idea or paragraph, I often took a coffee break and went down the basement to reset the dryer or toss another load in the washer. This particular time, while loading the washer, I saw Jason sitting beside the water tank, which was odd because I had just seen her two flights up, sitting on the old steamer trunk.

"Well, are you coming up?" I demanded. As she seemed content to stay where she was and I was impatient to get back to my work, I left her there to hunt, explore or just sit in the darkness. I had other things on my mind and knew I'd be back down to do more laundry in another hour or so.

But when I got back upstairs, there was Jason sitting on the steamer trunk. Doing a double take, thinking maybe I ought to lay off fiction for a while, I marked her indolent inertia and raced back to the basement—where Jason was still crouched beside the water tank!

Jason was a skinny shorthaired gray cat with greenish eyes, and I had not seen another all-gray cat since we'd left Ann Arbor. Upon closer examination, the cat by the water tank was a skinny all-gray cat with *yellowish* eyes. Where it came from or how it got in our basement I had not the foggiest all-gray idea, but in chortling amazement I instantly dubbed it *Mason*, brought it some food and water, then left it where it was.

When Bobbie got home, I whisked her upstairs to show her Jason still on the steamer trunk. Bobbie sighed, "Poor thing, at least she comes out once in a while."

Then whisked her to the basement and pointed to the gray cat.

"I don't understand—what's going on?"

"*Mason*," I said.

For several months we had two gray cats, and that was that. We let Mason come up from the basement, but we did not let him go upstairs into Jason's realm, and at night we returned him to the basement where we fed him and supplied him with a cat box. Unlike Jason, Mason went outside occasionally, but only out the back door, since he had no interest in dealing with Star.

One day, Mason went out and didn't come back; but—as the New Year's Eve salamander had—he left an indelible gray area in our family lore.

· 25 ·

CHICKEN JUSTICE

Also part of our family lore was "The Stupids." This came from Bobbie. She loved reading to Zack from a series of books about a family called "The Stupids," the book she most relished being *The Stupids Step Out,* and whenever any (or all) of us did anything especially foolish or silly they were likely to be greeted with some affectionate indignity like "Oh, just great, here we go: The Stupids Step Out!"

Our first bout with chickens epitomized the syndrome. When we'd bought the chickens for two dollars apiece, the lady had told us that they were old, but that hadn't meant much to us then. In the egg-collecting joy of that first endless summer, we just thought it meant something like getting two dozen a week instead of four dozen; and even if in fall and winter that dwindled further to one dozen or half a dozen, it would still have been more than we needed, more than enough to justify the silly fun of dealing with their dumb-cluck ways.

Everyone told us that in winter the egg production would drop off some, but if you kept the chicken house moderately cozy and installed artificial lights, it would fool them enough to keep them laying. We didn't have any electricity in the barn back then, so lights were out; but we brought in old blankets and extra hay bales and hoped that that would be enough to keep them going. It wasn't. By the end of November, they had stopped laying altogether; and by still-eggless March, our affection for them had waned considerably. Like gamblers trying to get even, we kept telling ourselves that we'd just have to recoup our losses later on.

Come spring, however, even though there was some slight resumption in egg production, the pace had slackened to the point where we were only getting a few eggs a week. When we asked old Mrs. Gee, the egg lady down the road, what we were doing wrong, she said they were probably just old and ready for the stewpot.

While it was dim of us, this revelation shocked us somewhat. We had imagined fewer eggs, but we hadn't contemplated chicken menopause, a point when they would simply be too old to ovulate, and that followed by chicken geriatrics—but, in fact, these hens were so far along that in midsummer two of them dropped dead of old age! Even so, we continued to limp along with them until late autumn, when their egg production had again dribbled off to zero. We finally decided that their time had come.

Our main reason for procrastination was that neither of us had ever been much as killers. As a boy I'd killed a bird or two with my BB gun, but killing had never been part of my upbringing. I'd always ended up feeling terrible about it. Perhaps that's why my being present at Ahog's slaughter and our personal butchering of Midnight had seemed so necessary. Unlike my boyhood experiences—which had only been to prove myself— on the farm it seemed essential to face the practical reality that meat in fact came from living animals, that there was something extremely hypocritical and cowardly about eating meat while denigrating hunters and butchers—as though they were somehow less evolved while we were too enlightened and superior to dirty our hands with such barbarities. Not that I ever felt the need to provide all our own meat—and I certainly didn't feel any need to take a bite out of the freshly killed still-warm heart of anything—but at least being willing to kill and pluck our own chickens did seem like a natural and necessary part of the progression.

Nonetheless, I continued to put it off until further delay became completely unjustifiable—after an unusually heavy early-December storm suddenly hit us with a foot of snow! What were we doing? Still trudging out to the milkhouse, breaking ice in the waterer, scattering feed, vitamins and oyster shells—the oyster shells to strengthen the shells of the eggs, of which there had been none for weeks!

The day after the storm, I sharpened my hatchet and went out with a stout oak plank. What I was remembering were those pictures that we used to color back in third and fourth grade at James Monroe Elementary School in South Bend, Thanksgiving pictures of Pilgrims cheerily putting turkeys on the chopping block. I had heard of wringing chickens' necks, but somehow that seemed too vicious and direct. Meanwhile, as I bundled up to do my part, Bobbie put a large canning kettle on to boil; we had read that dunking a bird in boiling water facilitated the plucking.

It was very cold—near zero—and, in the rarefied air, the nauseating stench in the cooped-up milkhouse further convinced me that I was doing the right thing. As the foul air was still laden with emotion, I further distanced myself by noting the bloody wounds on the chickens' rear quarters—caused by the disgusting way that they maintained their pecking order by attacking each other from behind, then pecking continually at each other's open wounds whenever they could.

I didn't know how, but somehow they seemed to know what I was there for. I expected them to rush around my feet like they always did when I came to feed them, but this time they began fluttering away from me and squawking in panic before I got a good chance to grab one. Finally I caught one in a corner and latched hold of its neck.

How easy it would have been to wring its neck right then, but I already had my other plan set in mind and I hardly considered it. I also thought that if the others witnessed the act, it would certainly make them even harder to catch. So, with my heart thumping brutally, I took the chicken out into the deep snow where I had laid the plank and left the hatchet, thinking only that I wanted to do a quick clean job and get it over with.

Unlike the Pilgrim pictures, however, the chicken did not nicely lay its neck upon the block. It took considerable man-handling before I got it in place with one hand and managed to reach the hatchet with the other. Another thing that hadn't occurred to me was that—while the oak plank was indeed rigid and sturdy for the task—the foot of snow beneath the plank was most soft and forgiving. So, when I brought the hatchet down forcefully, the underlayer of snow cushioned the blow. Instead of severing the chicken's head, I merely inflicted an ugly gash on its neck. As it squawked in pain, I screamed at myself: "For God's sake be quick about it and do it *right!*" Frantic and embarrassed, I pressed the chicken down to the board and lowered the hatchet with all my might—bringing it down not on the chicken's neck, but squarely on my thumb! I was wearing thick winter gloves and didn't know how much damage I had done; but from the feel of it, I could only imagine that my thumb was now quite possibly separated from my hand.

Cursing my clumsiness and stupidity, I hacked at the poor squawking chicken until its eyes went blue and its head also looked like a severed thumb. Rushing to the house, I presented Bobbie with the headless bird and hurried to the bathroom. I didn't want to tell Bobbie anything until I knew the extent of what I'd done. My hands were now too numb from the cold to feel much pain. With my heart in my mouth I slowly peeled off the blood-soaked glove and saw that my thumb was still my thumb—oozing badly and too bone-bruised to bend, but definitely still connected to my hand.

"What are you doing?" Bobbie called from the kitchen. "How did it go? I'm sure it was hard."

As I described what had happened, the dead bird in the boiling pot began to reek with the foulest stench we'd ever smelled.

"Let's just give it to Star," Bobbie said.

"No, goddamn it—after what I just went through we're going to *eat* the sonofabitch!" I certainly didn't want to have killed it for nothing.

Stupidity upon stupidity. We had also never thought that, *of course*, dunking and plucking was a thing that needed to be done *outside!* We were so concerned about my thumb, the killing, and accomplishing the plucking that, by the time the chicken was half-plucked, the fulminating skunky smell had permeated every corner and lath crack in the house before we realized our foolishness and got the potted bird out into the yard to work on the pinfeathers. Coming back inside from the pure cold air, we were practically folded over by the stench. The putrid wet feathers were still where we'd stuffed them in a paper bag, and strewn over whatever they'd stuck to.

Still persevering, after cleaning and Lysoling the kitchen, we stewed the chicken, leaving all the doors and windows open to the arctic air while it simmered. Then we attempted to eat it. I think its inedibility had less to do with its stringy toughness and actual flavor than with overcooked emotions and acrid associations. In any case, Star ended up with it, after all.

The next day we called "Hotline," a flea market and opinion show on the local radio station—one of Yates County's most popular programs—and offered a bunch of antiquated hens free to anyone who would come get them. An old man with a Polish name came for them, thanking us profusely and saying that he surely ought to be paying us something. We once again explained that they were tough old birds that didn't lay anymore.

"Best eatin' there is," he chortled. "Can't hardly find 'em like that no more!"

We were so happy to be rid of them that we went out to celebrate. He was so happy to get them that he showed up at the door again a few days later with a whole grocery bag full of spaghetti squash, venison sausage, and jars of homemade horseradish and chutney.

"Just felt too guilty 'bout takin' them hens for free. The wife fricasseed one up for Sunday dinner. Sure beats t'hell out of them things they sell for chickens nowadays."

· 26 ·

QUILLS—OR, WHERE'S JAMES HERRIOT WHEN YOU REALLY NEED HIM?

We had never seen a porcupine on our land, but one daybreak Star showed up with a mouth full of quills. At first we feared she might be rabid or in mid-seizure because she was frothing at the mouth so badly, her whole body shivering spasmodically, then lurching forward as she emitted a grotesque clacking from her snarling mouth. As we approached carefully, we saw three-and four-inch quills protruding from her muzzle like pins in a voodoo doll. Every time she lurched to the ground and swiped madly with her large paws, she broke off a few of the quills and drove them in even farther.

Despite the agonizing distraction, when she saw us she tried to give us her normal friendly greeting, ears lying back submissively, tail trying to wag, but the look in her small tawny eyes quickly eroded to a plea for help. I hurried for a pair of needlenose pliers and we took turns, one trying to hold her steady, the other trying to extract the quills one at a time, but—like fishhooks—the quills were tipped viciously with one-way barbs, each of them forcing Star to wince and shiver as it was twisted and ripped free from her nose, lips, cheeks or gums. While we did the best we could, a few of the quills broke off. Worse yet, as we worked our way farther in, we saw that the inside of her mouth and tongue were skewered similarly: the source of *clacking* was those interior quills raking against her teeth every time she moved her mouth.

Bravery and loyalty two of her most indomitable traits, Star never snapped or growled. Nonetheless, her bear-trap jaws kept tightening reflexively well beyond our strength to keep them safely open. Realizing the seriousness of the situation, we hoisted her into the back of the pickup, and while Bobbie stayed home with Annie and Zack, I drove as fast as the old truck would go to our usual vet in Penn Yan. But Doc McCarthy's wife told me that he was out of town and sent me on to another vet on the other side of town. By now Star was shaking badly and gagging for breath. It was still only about 7:00 A.M. After much knocking on the door of the second vet's house, his wife finally opened the door enough to tell me that the clinic wasn't open yet and that I'd have to wait while the doctor finished breakfast. I explained Star's situation frantically and she said she'd pass on the information. I got into the back of the truck with Star and tried my best to calm both of us down. It was at least fifteen or twenty minutes before the doctor finally emerged from the house, wiping the last few greasy crumbs from his mouth.

"The clinic doesn't open until 8:30," he grumbled, waving at the sign on the door. "Well—bring him in, I guess." Looking vaguely in my direction, not even glancing at Star, he pulled out some keys, unlocked the door to the clinic and went in.

Star hated vet clinics, and it took all my adrenaline strength to overcome her balking and haul her into the waiting room. The doctor had now disappeared behind a locked interior door through which I could hear him talking on the telephone.

When I banged on the door, he opened it curtly, took a quick look at Star and said, "Hm, really got into it, didn't he? We'll have to put him under—bring him in and set him on the table." And then went back to the telephone.

While I grasped Star and fumbled her up onto the examination table, the doctor was giving instructions to a farmer about his cows. Cradling the receiver under his neck and shoulder, he filled a syringe, set the phone down just long enough to stick the needle into a vein in Star's nearest sprawled leg and said, "Push the plunger in slowly until the syringe is empty—I'll be with you in a minute." Then returning to complete the instructions he was giving over the phone, he set up an appointment at the dairy farm for later that morning.

It felt like my own teeth clacking as I tried to cap my fulminating emotions and squeamishly pushed my thumb against the cold plastic plunger. For an instant, I had the terrible thought that maybe this was going to put her to sleep *permanently*. I looked at the doctor and he motioned brusquely for me to go ahead. "Uh, what is this—anesthetic?" I stammered. The doctor gestured to me with a sarcastic—*Yes, of course, what do you think?*—look.

"Okay, old girl—" I muttered, trying not to think what I might do if this Doctor of Apathy messed this up.

As soon as the anesthetic hit Star's bloodstream, her taut muscles sagged and her gagging for breath settled to a shallow breathing; clearly she was still alive. After another few minutes, finally the vet came over.

"Sorry you had to wait," he said, never looking at me but immediately picking up the quill-extracting job where we'd left it off. "Nothing against pets, but out here farm animals have to come first—this family's whole livelihood is hanging in the balance."

"Is she going to be all right?" I asked.

"*She?*"

"Star—my *dog!*"

"*She*, huh? Hm—big female."

"Will she be all right?"

"I don't see why not. A few of these broken barbs may fester, but they'll eventually work themselves out, I imagine. She might not feel much like eating for a few days. Be a while, I guess, before she takes on another porcupine."

Finally beginning to feel some relief, I mulled over what the doctor had said about pets versus farm animals. While it in no way excused his rudeness and insensitivity, I understood what he meant. Pets in the country were always coming and going, but a good milk cow wasn't so easy to come by.

When the doctor had finished, he scribbled out a bill for $40. I realized that in my panic I had left home without my wallet. When I started to explain, he launched into a tirade about all these new city people with their pets; not only expecting to be coddled, but then expecting him to do his job just for the fun of it.

Amazingly, Virginia Gibbs suddenly popped her head through the door from the waiting room, said she couldn't help overhearing, and held out two twenty-dollar bills in my direction, which I accepted gratefully and handed to the doctor. For her sake I resisted the urge to wad them up and bounce them off his surly nose. On my way out, with Star's weight leadening my arms and back, I paused to thank Virginia again, embarrassedly assuring her that I'd get the money back to her that afternoon. When I asked her how her family was, she winced. Then, with a painful shrug and terrible sigh, she said she was surprised I hadn't heard that her husband had died of a stroke just a few weeks before. That's why she was here, to have her herd of Jerseys inspected so that she could get on with selling them.

Going home, my head was a whirlpool. I thought of Virginia, the Gibbs children and the dairy herd with no one to tend them. The surly doctor was right, of course. How little Star should have mattered in comparison. Yet I realized that my overriding emotion was relief that Star was going to be all right. By the time I turned up the shortcut through Crystal Valley, the thing unavoidably began shaping and distancing itself into fiction—the twists, turns, barbs and conflicting values. A few months later, I wrote the story and called it "Quills," the second of four farm stories that I sold eventually to *Redbook*. Somehow, when I began writing these stories, it never occurred to me that they would have much local impact, but word always got around and each of them always became something of an event. None like "Quills," though. Locally, almost nobody bothered with the distinction that these incidents had been transformed into *fiction*. Specifically, many people not only recognized a resemblance to Virginia Gibbs, but also uncovered my model for the less-than-affable vet. In fact, I heard that the vet had received so many unwanted comments that he was considering suing me for libel.

I must confess that I tried to take solace from this, retribution for the doctor's rudeness, but instead it nettled me—not only because Star was now perfectly all right, but because in my story, far from vilifying the doctor, I'd thought I'd pretty much let him off the hook.

· 27 ·

JOKER AND STAR

We had a number of Ann Arbor and Iowa City friends who moved to the country about the same time we did, to: southern Missouri, northern Michigan, eastern Washington, central Maine. I guess when it came down to it, none of us were really very much the "commune" type. Despite the wide dispersal, most of us generally kept track of each other—at least while the children were still young—occasionally even making visits to each other's farms.

During most of the '70s, our closest friends, Ransom and Rosie, were renting a farm just past a wide curve outside of Nixa, Missouri. In many ways, they had been our models. They not only preceded us to the country by a year and started their family before us; but, as they'd both been raised in Texas and brought up with true rural connections, they were also the ones who taught us many of our first country skills. Ransom not only taught me how to use an ax and a chainsaw, he honed my ability to see. Having grown up hunting and trapping and using the woods, he showed me different kinds of tracks and scat, which kinds of wood were easy to split and good to burn, and where deer had bedded down or rubbed the bark off branches.

Because his father was a building contractor, Ransom also knew a lot about building and fixing, wiring and plumbing, roofing and floor finishing—all those house-essential activities that, in my youth, had been accomplished by "calling someone" and keeping out of the way.

Similarly, Rosie knew about things like finding wild asparagus and canning vegetables, stripping furniture, caning chairs and bargaining at flea markets. At that time, she had just opened a little antique store in Nixa. When I came upon some neighbors of ours with a barnful of old furniture that they wanted to unload cheaply, it became a wonderful excuse for a back-and-forth trip. Agreeing that we'd split the expenses and profits, Ransom flew up to our place, whereupon we loaded the best of the not-quite antiques into a 30-foot U-Haul and drove it back down to Nixa. Eventually we made back enough money to pay for all the tripping back and forth—and a little more, I think (though Bobbie says no).

In any case, for two weeks or so, we had a wonderful time. On the last day, after the furniture had finally been unloaded, sorted and stored in various places, we indulged ourselves in an all-day-and-most-of the-night celebration. Sometime around the Hour of the Wolf, Ransom finally crashed. But I was still buzzing. For a while we had sat on his porch to watch a terrific electrical storm, until the wind had shifted and driven us inside to carry on with the Stones and Beatles, Dylan and Neil Young.

After Ransom had gone under, my eyelids were still dancing on the windowpanes. I was still listening to the howling storm and trying to unwind the rest of the way down when I heard a scratching at the window, then suddenly saw a puppy's head, drenched and shivering, peering dolefully in at me.

In my present state of quasi-mind, more than unignorable —it seemed destined.

Several times Ransom had told me that because they lived just past the big curve at the edge of town, it was not unusual for them to find the remains of unwanted litters of kittens and puppies that people had dumped there. Like so much dirt swept under the rug; out of sight, out of mind. Maybe their "owners" thought it was better than shooting or drowning them; this way—if they somehow survived, if someone took them in . . . But it was not only unconscionable, it was extremely unneighborly. Several times Ransom and Rosie had awakened to one or several puppies or kittens in their yard, predictably followed by a fight with their children who always wanted to keep them, of course. That was followed by the further unpleasantness of taking them to the pound in nearby Springfield.

Most of the poor things, if they weren't hit right there by cars coming around the curve, if they didn't drown in the creek that ran under the road, or if they weren't taken by dogs or hawks or owls, died of starvation or exposure in the tick-laden thickets or open fields. On this particular electrical night of deluge and discovery, most of this puppy's littermates had probably drowned. It seemed a miracle that this one could have gotten this far. So pathetic but such a survivor! Finding him utterly irresistible, I brought him inside, dried him off and fed him. For quite a while Bobbie and I had been talking about getting another dog as a companion for Star.

"We'll call it Joker," I once told her (I'd been listening to a lot of Dylan). "What do you think—Joker and Star?"

An hour or so later, when Rosie got up with baby Xan, she was amazed to find me still up—and with a *dog!*

"This is Joker," I said. "He came to me in the night."

Rosie shook her head laughing. "I know it was raining cats and dogs, but this is ridiculous!"

I took Joker home with me on the plane. He peed on me in the St. Louis airport (where I had taken him out of his travel box during a two-hour layover). When Bobbie picked me up in Rochester, I presented her with the shaggy-dog story and the shaggy dog. She also found Joker instantly irresistible. Everyone found Joker irresistible. He was as irresistible as he was footloose and fancy free—a born wanderer, aptly named.

Although Star tended to maul Joker a little bit from time to time, they generally got along well. In many ways, Joker grew up looking like a miniature Star. They were similar in shape and coloring. If Star was a female who looked like a giant he-wolf, then Joker was a male who was slight and delicate, like a fox. But that was as far as the similarity went. In temperament, as loyal and stalwart as Star was, that's exactly how undependable and disloyal Joker was.

We got Joker neutered as soon as he was old enough, but he still continued to wander, often disappearing for days at a time. Especially because Star roamed free, we didn't have the heart to tie him up. During one of his longest absences, we even heard through the school-bus grapevine that he was being kept by another family. We were just starting to adjust to that fateful quirk—thinking that we had named him *Joker*, after all—when he came back to us, as affable as ever. That I'd saved his unfaithful little life and dragged him all the way back from the foothills of the Ozarks meant nothing to him. He was like a dandy little traveling minstrel. We also knew he spent a lot of time with the basement-dwelling family we'd got Ahog from, and after a while he seemed to be almost as much their dog as ours.

Then one day, one of that family's children who rode the school bus with Zack told him that Joker had gotten into their chickens—and their father had shot him. I never forgave the man for that, but in my heart I knew the fault was nearly as much ours as his. Or nobody's. Joker had simply been one of those ramblin', gamblin', shiftless, whimsically born-to-be-wild, you-had-to-love-him country-song souls who was bound to live life on his own terms: Joker from Day One.

· 28 ·

NAMELESS PIGS

Keuka College, where Bobbie taught psychology for two years, was a small women's college surrounded by rolling farms and vineyards on three sides and fronted by Keuka Lake on the fourth. Keuka Lake, because of its regal setting and graceful shape, was called "Queen of the Finger Lakes." Keuka College, because of its financial woes, was reluctantly on the verge of matriculating men in a desperate effort to survive.

Even after Bobbie quit teaching to become a clinical psychologist at Elmira Psychiatric Center, the college continued to feed us in various ways. For instance, I occasionally taught adjunct English courses there and became a regular in the noontime basketball game at Weed Physical Arts Center. In the locker-room chatter after one of those games, one of the other adjunct teachers, who heard that we lived on a farm, said he and his wife were just moving out of a farmhouse and still had two young pigs. Then he proposed that they would pay all expenses and give us half the meat—*if* we would raise them.

It seemed too good a deal to turn down.

And, in fact, I suppose it was a good deal. He showed up one Saturday in a borrowed truck with a couple of young 50- or 60-pound Poland China pigs, and eight months later came back to pick up half the 400 pounds of hanging pork. This was our first experience in raising food for someone else. As a result, and maybe because the image of pigs as cultural icons had pretty much played out by then, these two animals never really meant much more to us than meat on the cloven hoof. We never even named them. Maybe some of it had to do with the unclear ownership, which was somewhat absurd—after all, what does a pig care about "ownership"?—but somehow it did matter that we never quite saw them as *ours*.

Certainly, we fed them well and weren't unkind. That there were *two* of them was also significant—not only because it made them harder to individualize, but even more because it brought out a certain swinish competitiveness that made them considerably less lovable. Ahog, by himself, had been very cozy in his sugar-shack-converted pig house, comfortably burying himself in the provided straw bedding, unquestionably pigging out on whatever food we supplied, but never to the point of being destructive. These two, however—each always trying to hog all the food and space for itself—tore apart the trough still left from Ahog, rooted up and smashed the pig house floorboards, constantly wreaked havoc on the barnboard fencing. Each time I built them a bigger, stronger trough, they smashed that, too. When I built two individual troughs, they ruined them both. Eventually, we fed them in a large metal tub; but, even then, when their food was gone, they often kicked it away or turned it over with their snouts, tossed it into the muddy center of the pen or into the sloppy corner they used for excrement.

Maybe if we had felt differently about them from the beginning—if we had named them—they would have been less like that. But I doubt it. More likely, it was just their piggishly competitive nature made worse by their penned up confine-ment. Whatever the porcine psychology of it, we felt we'd earned the meat and decided that from then on we would raise only animals of our own.

· 29 ·

KITTY AND SHIVER

When Zack was five, for two straight mornings he complained at breakfast that he couldn't sleep because he heard a kitten meowing in the woods. The first morning we told him it was probably just a catbird, a bird that got its name because its call sounded so much like a cat. Zack gave us a wide-eyed skeptical look, as if maybe this was another one of those imaginary things that parents needed to tell kids, so we got out the Audubon bird book and showed him what a catbird looked like.

"That doesn't look anything like a cat!"

"No, but it *sounds* like a cat," I said. In fact, it looked more monklike than catlike in its gray robe color and black skullcap.

"But this sounded like a little kitten."

"Well, sometimes catbirds sound like kittens, too. *Mew! Mew!* —just like that."

"Why do they sound like kittens?"

"I'm not sure, but maybe it's a way of keeping other birds and little animals away from their nests. If the egg stealers think there's a cat around, maybe they're so afraid that it keeps them away."

"Why don't they sound like *real BIG* cats, then?"

"Hmm, well—let's see. Good question. Well, maybe I'm wrong. Maybe that's just the kind of sound they make—the way crows go *caw caw*, and pigeons go *coo-coo*. The truth is, I don't really know why they sound like kittens. But they do—I know that."

"This really *really* REALLY sounds like a kitten!"

The second morning, when Zack was so insistent about the kitten that he even kept on about it despite missing his Saturday morning cartoons, we took him out to see what we could find—me carrying two year-old Annie in our blue canvas backpack, Bobbie and Zack hurrying ahead hand in hand.

We were hardly a quarter-mile down the road when we all heard the kitten. Bobbie spotted it on a low branch of a double poplar. I was able to get at it by stepping in the low crotch where the twin trunks joined and pulling the cat-laden branch within reach, my one foot still hanging in the air as I worked my hand under the belly of the trembling little all-black furball, its twenty tiny claws transferring to my branch-supplanting wrist, Annie already climbing up my neck trying to grab it. After determining it was female, we gave Zack the honor of naming her; he chose Kitty Coffman.

Shiver came two years later by way of the day-care center. One of the workers there had slyly shown up one day with a box full of kittens which she'd let the children play with, then gave the kids "free kittens" notes to take home. A surer bet than dealing three-card monte, the kittens were all gone in a day or two. Knowing we were hopelessly had, Bobbie drove Zack and Annie to the woman's barn that same night. Annie grabbed up a tiny fluffy male tabby which shivered so much in her arms on the way home that she named him Shiver.

At the time we'd definitely felt suckered by the woman, but Shiver became such a wonderful pet that—two years later, when Kitty Coffman had her kittens—Bobbie used a similar strategy to give our kittens away. She took them down to the Dundee Street Fair in a brightly colored box that soon emptied.

In those days we always let our female pets have one litter before getting them spayed. This had even been true with Jason in Ann Arbor. Unfortunately, it had been while my college freshman sister Jeannie was house-sitting for Bobbie that Jason gave premature birth to her kittens and—to Jeannie's horror—*ate* them! Although Jeannie braved the trauma and even tried to make light of it, that was forever it with Jeannie and cats. And while it was hard to see that the experience had been of much benefit to Jason, either, we still somehow felt it important to let Star and Kitty Coffman have their litters, too. As time passed, however, that "importance" came to seem more and more like an embarrassing vestige of romantic youth in a world that had far more kittens than it was willing to take care of.

For the next dozen years—almost exactly coincidental with Zack and Annie's school years at Dundee—Kitty and Shiver became our two most personable house pets. From the beginning, Zack remained partial to Kitty and Annie to Shiver, each continuing to sleep every night with their favorite, K–12. While the two cats themselves did not get along particularly well, they tolerated each other. Shiver, much larger, often chased Kitty until she had enough, and then a quick claw in the face always put things back in order. Of all our animals, Shiver was the most lovable, Kitty the most resourceful.

Shiver existed less as a personality than as an *entity* of lavish self-pleasure and trusting affection. Much of the time he was hardly more than a mohair-soft throw pillow, sprawling unabashedly on the nearest lap, purring loudly to be scratched and petted. He was so content within his own skin that he often stretched out on his back, hanging half off of the sofa, bed or chair. He was so trusting that if he fell he didn't even bother to twist and land on his feet in typical cat fashion—but merely plopped to the floor like dead pillow weight, cushioned safely by his utter relaxation and stupidity; whereupon, jarred by the rudeness of reality, he usually just shook his head at the insult, licked himself for good measure, and then stretched himself out wherever he'd landed and returned to thoughtless bliss. Needless to say, Shiver wasn't much of a hunter. Outside, he often pretended to be a cat: prowling and stalking, ridiculously noncamouflaged in his bright orange-and-white fur. Every now and then he amazed himself by actually catching a mouse—if he happened on one even dumber than he was.

In the house, Shiver was so passive that for several weeks

one winter there was a mouse actually eating cat food right out of his dish—right *within* his dreamy purview! We didn't know whether to laugh or be appalled. It was almost embarrassing. Here we were in our illusions of country practicality, not only buying cat food for this useless cat, but also for the kitchen mouse that the cat was supposed to catch. We kept Shiver's dish on the floor next to the stove. Presumably this tiny mouse, hardly bigger than my big toe, lived somewhere in the warmth behind the stove. In winter, that was always one of the places where Bobbie set out a flat yellow container of d-Con, as well as in the closet crawl spaces, attic and basement. She had a loathing fear of rats, and even the mice were real pests in the cupboards. And at night, hearing them scurrying in the walls, I also worried about them chewing on the old wiring or nesting in our bagged-up extra blankets and clothes. Less reluctant to set out poison in the house than I was, Bobbie mostly took it upon herself to control the in-house rodent population.

This little mouse was different, though. Once past the shock of seeing him reach up over the lip of Shiver's dish, I made a plea for him. No matter how cute he was, Bobbie could never quite accept the idea of a mouse running free in her kitchen, but I was so taken by its brazen cheek that I convinced her to let it be.

"So, we'll have a pet mouse for a while. Obviously, it doesn't have to gnaw into the Quaker Oats and Cheerios when it's got a free lunch right here." I didn't ask her to remove the d-Con, though. There was also the likelihood of its running into Kitty some night. After a week or two, the nervy little thing was gone.

Kitty Coffman was night-and-day different from Shiver—nervous, skinny, wily and untrusting—as one might have expected from her early abandonment, followed by tree-trapped days and nights. And who knew how many lives she used up getting that far? In any case, the pattern was set. As if the two had been color-coded according to their personalities, Shiver was clownishly extroverted, a splash of orange-and-white; and Kitty was dark, wary, and street-wise—even into the cratered uncertainty of her half-moon yellow eyes. While Kitty was not as neurotic and reclusive as Jason, she had many of the same tendencies. She rarely came to anyone's lap and when she did she was always stiff and kneady, wanting affection but barely allowing it, muscles taut, short black fur almost brittle to the touch, forever fidgeting, trying to climb to the top of one's neck, digging her claws in—*forcing* one to shoo her away. Inexplicably, it was often the laps of people who disliked cats that Kitty sought out most, like my father's. My father had a phobia about cats, so we always tried to keep the cats upstairs or outside when my parents were visiting. But invariably, at least once every visit, Kitty managed to jump on my father's lap or onto the couch beside him, suddenly kneading her claws into his arm or shoulder before we could seize her and toss her out.

It was only Zack whom Kitty truly trusted, and only he who truly tried to fulfill her kinky and unlikably cloying needs for affection.

Kitty was a complainer, her weak reluctant purr like a distant motor, like the pump running in the basement; but when she really wanted something, she vociferously and incessantly meowed until attention was paid—a trait that more than once reminded us of Bobbie's father.

Shiver's meowing was always vaguely plaintive, as though he knew he wanted something but couldn't quite figure out what it was. When Shiver was hungry, he meowed at the sky as though expecting manna to drop from heaven. But Kitty was specific: if she was hungry, she meowed at the old woodbox where we kept the cat food; if she wanted to go out, she meowed at the corner of the door. Kitty figured things out. She figured out how to unlatch the door so she could come upstairs. One of her favorite places to lie was on the fresh towels in the bathroom closet. In order to reach those high open shelves, she had to climb the toilet, jump to the windowsill and then jump several feet at an angle up to the towels.

We were not very happy with this, of course, so I built doors to close off the shelves. Then Kitty learned how to climb onto the ledge above the shelves, reach down to open the doors, then go back to the windowsill and leap onto the towels. So I put a latch on the doors. And Kitty figured out how to undo the latch. So, I put on a *better* latch! So instead, she took to jumping from the washbasin to the top of the bathroom door and onto the upper shelf on the other side, where we kept extra sheets and blankets.

Of all her tricks, the most exasperating by far was when I was upstairs trying to write and Kitty wanted to come in from outside. Knowing that I couldn't hear her meowing, she learned that by climbing up on the roof of the woodshed that sloped right up to my writing window, she could meow in my face until I either had to go outside and climb a ladder to bring her in from the roof, *or* open my writing window so that she could run in across my desk, leaving snowy or muddy catprints on my papers. Eventually, I learned to make sure that she was always inside during my writing hours. With Kitty, it always seemed that we were having to adjust our behavior to hers.

One morning, when Kitty was four or five, I took a break from my writing and found her staggering around in the upstairs hallway. Her yellow eyes rolling around like two crazily spinning tops, she suddenly keeled over on her side. Blood began oozing from her ear. The vet called it "some kind of cerebral event," a seizure that would most likely repeat itself and probably do her in fairly soon. There was nothing to be done, he said, but since she wasn't suffering, neither was there any urgency unless we didn't want to deal with the unpleasantness of it.

As she was already pretty much the embodiment of unpleasantness, we decided that we might as well keep her. And, in fact, Kitty recovered completely, never had another "cerebral event," and remained as crotchety and resourceful as ever for another ten or eleven years.

· 30 ·

CHICKENS II

Our friend George the artist was living with a new woman named Dotty, a hairdresser from Dundee. Every two or three years it seemed that George had a new woman living with him. We knew he'd had three or four wives, at least, and at least two other women since the last wife—Joy—had left the first year we'd arrived. One day Bobbie and I were ribbing George about his "artist's way with women."

"It's not that I ever wanted it that way," he protested painfully. "They just always leave."

At that time, George was about fifty. Unlike any of his previous women whom we'd met, Dot was about his age, a woman with a real country background and not in any way involved with the arts. They were almost like a middle-aged country couple, except for the decor of George's kinetic machines, wind sculptures, fantastic fountains, nontimekeeping clocks, paintings, masks, purple refrigerator and a woodburning stove that he'd fashioned into something that looked like a fabulistic tuba. Other than that, George had a very nice vegetable garden, several hives of honeybees and a coopful of chickens.

Our children always loved to visit George's, as did we. He always had four or five beautiful and amazing things that we hadn't seen before. One spring, George gave us a basket of newly hatched chicks. Dotty put a dot of food coloring on each of their fluffy heads, each a different color so that Zack and Annie could tell them apart and name them. At home, I built them a little wire coop behind the woodshed, but the next day the coop was destroyed and the chicks were gone. When we found Star with yellow fluff in her whiskers, I was so furious that I beat her with a stick, holding the bit of fluff up to her, then hitting her some more. She acted like she knew what she'd done wrong, but I didn't know whether or not she really did.

I should have been beating myself for having trusted her and not foreseen this awful incident, but the pain in Zack's face was a greater punishment than any I took out on Star. Annie was only three and too young to make much of the loss, but Zack was quietly horrified. It was his quietness that fooled us. Zack was usually extremely open and verbal about his feelings, and we did not realize how deeply bothered he was. After some brief consolation, Bobbie and I had pretty much dismissed the whole thing as unfortunate and let it go at that. I don't think either of us had really been too enthusiastic about raising a brood of chicks right then anyway, which may have even been a factor in my lackadaisical efforts to adequately secure their protection.

But for Zack this was an emotional Mixmaster. While this was hardly his first introduction to death, he'd been only Annie's age or younger when Ahog and Tina and Midnight and our first chickens had all come and gone. But those animals had all somehow belonged to the farm, and these chicks had been given to him and Annie. This was his first experience with the death of something personally his. Even more disturbing was that Star had been the agent of this personal and irreversible loss. Zack adored Star. What was he supposed to think? For the first time, he had to encounter someone he loved doing an entirely hateful and unfixable thing.

The next day at show-and-tell time in his first-grade class, Zack suddenly began sobbing about his "poor little chickies." When his teacher called and told us, we talked it over with Zack in greater depth.

"Terrible things happen sometimes. It really isn't right to blame Star, though. Dogs are hunters by their nature; she didn't know how much they meant to you."

"Did she have to eat *all* of them!" Zack wailed.

It was two or three weeks before he forgave Star. For several nights, he had nightmares about the chicks. For a week or so, he kept a jar of fireflies on his bedstand to use as a night-light. For several months he kept Kitty tightly in his arms until he fell asleep.

· 31 ·

A MIGRATION
OF MONARCHS

Considering their initial misgivings, my parents were not long in making peace with the idea of our rural migration. Maybe in their best of all possible worlds, it wouldn't have been their first or second choice, but the horror of their first encounter—the sweltering Indian summer when baby Zack had been eating cluster flies—calcified quickly into the remoteness of family myth. It wasn't long before they even came to enjoy their yearly visits.

Zack and Annie were both healthy, loving and bright, and that was certainly the most encouraging factor. And each visit found the house and yard a bit less rough, a little easier for them to live with. Not only did we get electricity in our bathroom, allowing Dad to use the mirror and his electric shaver at the same time, but, as the years flowed, our old furniture slowly got refinished, the kitchen got redone, and we even built a rustic barn-wood deck that looked out over the garden and the pond.

The more my parents were able to relax, the more they began to appreciate the beauty of the farm. But I don't think they ever really felt the power and the magic of it until our eighth or ninth year there, the year that the monarchs came.

In early autumn, we always had a splurge of monarchs. By then, most of the fields and gardens had died down and only the heartiest of flowers remained: Queen Anne's lace and blue chicory bordering the road, the fields rolling in thick waves of goldenrod and purple wild asters. And at that same time— when most of the other butterflies had already laid their eggs and died—the monarchs began appearing by the dozens, some years by the hundreds. Instead of withering with the frost, the monarchs began to gather—eventually, somewhere, they gathered in tremendous numbers, got on their dancing shoes and commenced their amazing migration to central Mexico.

Because of their commonness, I sometimes took for granted how exquisitely beautiful monarchs were; then, somewhere near me—usually when I was immersed in some practical project—I'd suddenly see one light on a flower and open toward me in a moment of perfect grace, the sunlight glinting and glowing on its orange-and-black–patterned wings, its slightly trembling wings looking like living panes of stained glass.

For some reason, the monarchs also liked to settle on the roads—oblivious to the wheels and windshields of progress. Despite their beauty, while driving I usually made only a cursory effort to avoid hitting them—cursory because any attempt short of driving at Mennonite horse-and-buggy speed would have been futile anyway. There were so many of them; their swirling flight was so unpredictable, and they lacked the agility, acceleration and savvy of birds. But even as I tried to tell myself that they were only insects after all, I still always felt a twinge of hypocritical guilt whenever I splattered one—it always made me wonder what my hurry exactly was.

In South Bend my parents were certainly not unfamiliar with monarchs; but, when they arrived on that particular early

October visit, they said they'd never before seen them in such profusion as around our house. And, in fact, neither had we. On the second day of their visit, when we all took a stroll down the road after lunch to look at the trees in the peak of autumn change, the air was filled with hundreds of monarchs. I had never before realized how much they looked like swirling autumn leaves.

As Zack and Annie skipped ahead, the monarchs began fluttering up all around us. When we followed their flight, we discovered that even greater numbers of them had settled in the trees. In fact, the branches were *thick* with them as far up as we could see, their dark orange coloring so well camouflaged by the trees that we couldn't tell where the butterflies began and the shimmering leaves left off. Impulsively, I threw a pebble up into the trees, and suddenly it was as if the treetops themselves lifted up. Tens of thousands, if not *millions*, of monarchs rose up on both sides of the road in a great wave, a resplendent flurry of undulating color, and then the greater mass of them resettled in the trees, again disappearing into the dancing flutter of incandescent leaves.

It overwhelmed the eye and brain. Three generations of us gasped as one. To the adults, it seemed almost as alien as it was magnificent. Only Zack and Annie, dancing and laughing and leaping after them, wanting me to throw more pebbles, wanting to throw pebbles themselves (which I refused to allow), were young enough to accept it only as another wondrous natural event. So many miracles were still new to them: the brightly striped caterpillar that became a butterfly; the sticky milkweeds that were the monarch caterpillars' only food; the milkweeds' own cocoonlike pods that could be unzipped to release a multitude of silky magical puffs into the wind; the wind itself that was like the earth's breath.

We were all reduced to children, afloat in that elevated state.

All afternoon we kept going back out to see if they were still there, gaping and giggling anew until, finally, they were hidden by the dusk. The next morning, the leaves were still swirling and fluttering, but the butterflies were gone, every one of them. The magnificence remained, however, and for years to come my parents loved to tell of that wondrous thing that had happened on their visit to the farm.

We've since read several articles about migrations of monarchs—the only butterflies known to migrate—their Oaxacan destination almost 4,000 miles away! While it's not known how many of them survive the flight, it's thought that several generations of them live and die before their return. And yet, somehow, they not only return to the same area from which they came, but even follow the same flight pattern, including the same rest stops.

If indeed our woods had become an annual rest stop for the monarch migration, I think that maybe the experience might have eventually lessened into one of those old-hat miracles—like milkweeds and wind, metamorphosis and changing autumn leaves—but, as it was, they stopped in our woods only that one time.

·32·

SUBFAMILY:
HOUSEPET TEMPORARIA

Especially during Zack and Annie's grade-school years, we almost always had one or another inside pet besides the two cats. Most came in like osmosis, poor little outside creatures who suddenly found themselves on the ledge of the fieldstone fireplace in a jar, box, bowl or makeshift aquarium—accompanied by a couple native rocks, some clumps of grass, a saucer of water and a few dead flies. At one point Annie even had a jar of pet worms that she would take out and let crawl around. She had names for each of them, and Zack told us that she even thought about dressing them.

Basically, this subfamily fell into three categories:

1.   The Cute, The Ugly and The Slow—toads, tadpoles, turtles, snails, snakes, worms, etc.

2.   The Amazing and The Weird—praying mantises, walking sticks, katydids, lightning bugs, millipedes, cocoons, glowworms, etc.

3.   The Pathetic and The Wounded—birds that couldn't fly, anything that was more than half-dead.

The duration for this last category was almost always less than a day—with the exception of one broken-winged sparrow that was actually nursed for sufficient days to get it back into wobbly flight.

In categories 1 and 2, the duration sometimes extended to

a week or two, until terminated by death, merciful release, or escape.

Once, the day before Bobbie's parents arrived for a visit from Detroit, Zack caught two red-bellied snakes—one about eight inches long, the other a little bigger. Bobbie was hardly thrilled at having snakes in the living room, never mind with her *parents* coming—but as Zack had worked his Tupperware habitat into an especially charming little snakehouse just so he could show it off to Grandma and Grandpa, she decided to leave the project for them to see, despite her mother's squeamishness about snakes.

"Very interesting, dollink," Bobbie's mother Vera told Zack in her thick Bulgarian accent, as adoringly as she could, *considering*—"but pliz, Zacky . . . just kip them *in* the box and away from *me!*"

The next morning when, as usual, Vera got up early to make breakfast for everyone, Zack came rushing up to her in the kitchen.

"Grandma! Grandma! Guess what? You'll never guess what happened!"

"Hokay—you tell me."

"The big snake *ate* the little snake!"

"No, sweetie—I dun't know too much about snakes, but I rilly dun't think they do *that!*"

"Well, he *must* have—because the little snake's *Gone!*"

We jumped out of bed to Vera's screams and were soon making a thorough downstairs search for the missing smaller serpent—to no avail. Then we immediately took the remaining snake outside and implacably coaxed Zack into releasing it into the garden. Later, over pinochle, Vera suddenly began laughing and retelling the incident, which was already becoming one of her favorite stories.

For a while, we also had a real fish aquarium, a fairly expensive Hanukkah/Christmas present that the kids had begged for but quickly quit taking care of, and—after many fights about feeding and cleaning the tank, followed by a lugubrious procession of bellied-up angelfish, black mollies and toilet-flushing eulogies—one day, when the kids were in school, I dumped them all, and later truthfully said that they'd all died. There were a few tears and I felt a little sorry for the fish, but they were never really missed at all.

The hamsters were another story. From the mall pet store, under Bobbie's aegis, Zack got a tan male hamster that he named Arthur, and Annie got a white female that she named Snowflake, although she almost always called it Poozie. I was very grumpy about the hamsters. I never wanted them in the first place; but Zack and Annie loved them, and Bobbie had a cooing affection for them, too.

"I don't know, *poisoning* mice and *raising* hamsters in the same house seems crazy to me, like 'The Stupids Do *Rodents'!*"

"It's completely different. The hamsters aren't running wild in our cupboards and walls! God, you sound just like my father. Why should you care? The kids are taking care of them; nobody's asking *you* to do anything."

"Yeah, we'll see," I said quite prophetically, though at the time I was conceding reluctantly. I didn't really care that much. I just didn't believe hamsters capable of any real personal interaction or affection. To me, they were living creatures being treated like *toys*, their whole lives boxed and outfitted for human amusement. Of course they were kind of cute zipping around their little obstacle course and on their circuslike apparatuses, but there was something profane about the commercial use of animals for mere childish diversion.

One thing, though, the pair of hamsters did provide quite an object lesson in the cycle of life. They prolifically ran life's stages the same full-tilt way they ran the miniature circus wheel in their cage; hamster gestation being only fifteen days, newborns reaching sexual maturity in just eleven weeks.

Annie was ten. She was incredibly excited during Poozie's two-week pregnancy, so thrilled at the litter's birth that she registered the event right next to the height chart that we kept on the inside of the broom-closet door: *JULY 16, 1984, HAMSTER BABIES ARE BORN. 8 OF THEM.*

Suddenly we had ten hamsters instead of two. Knowing that when they were weaned the pet shop would gladly take them, we bargained with Annie, saying we'd let her keep them for two months—but then no complaining when it was time for them to go. We certainly didn't want to end up in the hamster business ourselves. In the meantime—as hands-on as Annie was—we also established two new rules: No handling the babies until they were weaned. No more than *one baby* out of the cage at a time.

One night, however, when she was cleaning the babies'

cage, she neglected to secure the latch. In the morning, all the hamsters were out and gone. By then they were three or four weeks old and about half-grown.

Annie was terribly afraid they were dead. I was even more afraid they were alive—*in the walls!* The hamster mathematics of it was this: 11 weeks to sexual maturity; 15-day gestation; average litter of 8 (half females) *equals* a new litter every 13 weeks—*compounded quarterly!*—due four times a year, like our car insurance—or, in the case of exponentially increasing rodents:

by Election Day, 32 more babies, 42 hamsters in all—21 females;

by Groundhog's Day, 210 hamsters—105 females;

by May Day, 1,050—525 females;

by July Fourth, 5,250—2,625 females;

in one year, 26,250-13,125 females;

in two years, 16,406,250—8,203,125 females;

in three years, over 10 BILLION—more than twice as many hamsters in our walls as people on earth! Talk about good insulation!

Fortunately, it didn't come to that. In fact, the next morning, I saw Kitty very alertly watching the metal cover over a section of the baseboard heating pipes. Then I heard the scampering of little feet. How easy it would have been for them to follow the pipes into the wall! But I hurried to the other end of the heating section, loosened the bottom cover, and out they came—one baby hamster, two baby hamsters, three, four—in a seeming miracle *all eight!*

And, indeed, the pet shop was very pleased to get them.

· 33 ·
CHICKENS III

When Zack was in the second grade and excitedly brought home a shoebox of chicks that his class had incubated, we faked some delight and wonder. Privately, we considered writing his teacher a letter, saying how inexcusably irresponsible it was for her to set up parents like that, forcing them into the choice either of raising chickens or of having to take them away from an excited seven-year-old. Upon further discussion with Zack, it came out that she had, at least, asked the children to obtain permission from home. But since we'd had chickens twice before, Zack had said that he already *knew* we'd want some. Which was hardly the case— the distasteful conclusions of our other two chicken episodes had hardly yet dissipated. However—given Zack's trauma over the chicks that Star had chomped the year before—we were heartened by his enthusiasm for another try.

This time, I revived the Star-proof space in the milk house that we had used with our first chickens. Even though Star seemed to have matured some in the past year and regarded these new chicks with concerted deference, there was no need to tempt her.

By midsummer, Zack's interest in the chickens had waned almost totally. By then, all eight of them had flourished into young adulthood, and every other day or so we began to get a beautiful egg. Even at that age, it was still not easy to tell an adolescent hen from an adolescent rooster. At some point during their maturation, Bobbie happened onto an article about "sexing chicks," an occupation that I had never thought of before, but one that in large chicken operations had great importance. After all, how many roosters did a chicken farm need? According to the article, when they were only a few days old, all of the chicks were put on a conveyor belt and run past "chicken sexers" who delicately felt into their fluffy nether parts and then diverted the females into egg slavery and the males to the fatten-for-fryers department. Because the job required such tremendous digital dexterity and tedium tolerance, it was very difficult to find workers with adequate skill and temperament. Mostly, it was a job done by young Asian women—because of their small hands, the article said.

Reading this article reached in and pinched me someplace where I didn't want to be pinched. Instantly, this job took its place among the Worst Jobs I'd Ever Heard Of, as I tried not to think what it would be like to spend half my waking life feeling up chicken gonads.

Of our eight chickens—judging mainly from the size and redness of beards and combs—we were fairly sure that we had three roosters and five hens. By summer's end, when we were still getting only a single egg at a time, and it was quite clear that we were feeding and cleaning up after at least three more roosters than we needed or wanted, we traded the three roosters with the biggest, reddest combs to old Mrs. Gee, the Egg Lady near Altay, in exchange for a couple dozen brown eggs.

And then our one egg stopped coming.

Some months later, Bobbie ran into Mrs. Gee, who told her

that one of the roosters we'd given her was a hen. By then, we were quite aware of that, as we were of the reality that—of the eight chicks that Zack had brought home, *seven* had been roosters, and we had given away our only laying hen! Bobbie asked Mrs. Gee if she could use five more young roosters. Mrs. Gee said not really but if we were giving them away she supposed she'd take them.

· 34 ·

PONY PRELUDE

In lieu of a Christmas letter one year, Ransom and Rosie sent us a Super-8 home movie. On that very nasty winter night, we built a big fire in the fireplace and cozied in to watch it, to a sound track of bitter howling winds rattling all our ill-fitting old windows and doors. The movie did not merely greet us with our Missouri friends mugging good wishes and looking well, its centerpiece showed off their children with a beautiful pair of Shetland ponies and a fancy little surrey to boot. Taken by complete surprise, we tried to affect the appropriate joy, but our burbling responses soon began to reflux with a jealous aftertaste. It wasn't so much the fact that they'd recently come into some money as it was that for the last year or so, Annie had been absolutely crazy to get a pony. Not that she was the first young girl to whimsically want a pony, but she was more reasonably tempted by the fact that our family already possessed an empty barn and a fenced-in pasture. Reacting to the movie, Bobbie and I discussed it. What would a pony cost? There was also the tack. And I'd have to build a stall and fix the fence. And there were vet and blacksmith costs to consider. And hay and oats to buy—horses required a better grade of hay than cows—better than what we had in our overgrown old hayfields.

And even if we could find the money, Annie was only eight. Was she old enough for that kind of responsibility, or would we just be setting her up for trouble? Our discussion ricocheted back and forth, each of us countering the other pro and con, vacillating until we finally let it go, the evening crimped unpleasantly with mixed feelings and frustration.

Anyway, it was senseless to give any serious thought to getting a pony before spring.

A few hours later that same night, around 10:30 or so, Star suddenly started barking. I ignored it for a few moments, until it was clear that she wasn't just barking at the storm. Something was definitely out there that she didn't like. Cupping my hands at the window, I looked for car lights in the driveway or in front of the house but could see nothing. Grumbling, I got a flashlight, threw on my hooded sheepskin coat, slipped on my gloves and snowmobile boots, went onto the porch and stared out into the flailing snow. Star was making such a fuss that Bobbie hurriedly threw on a heavy coat over her robe and nightgown, put on her duck boots, muffler and knit beret, and came out with me. As we walked from the flagstone path to the driveway, the flashlight was mostly useless for seeing anything beyond ourselves. The refraction created an aura that enveloped us like a strange accompanying bubble of light. When we got past the parked car and truck, we could dimly see

Star's thickly crouched form and hear the menacing growls between her bursts of frantic barking. I immediately called her to me, but she held her ground stubbornly.

I couldn't imagine who would be out on a night like this unless someone had had an accident. Once in a while someone went off the road around the big curve past the woods and showed up at our door, asking numbly to use the phone. One time some crazy fool had been cutting wood at *night*—stealing it, no doubt—and had come to the door with his whole leg laid open with a chain-saw wound. Or maybe it was just some kind of wounded or rabid animal that Star had at bay.

As soon as we got to the road, though, we saw two human figures huddled together, staying back and holding their distance. I quickly whacked Star and chased her back. Closer up, we saw an old man and a teenage boy, both bundled up in layers of shabby clothes and looking half-frozen.

"Are you all right? Did you have an accident?" Bobbie asked.

"I'm here with the pony," the old man said.

"*What?*"

"Got this-here pony!" The two of them stepped aside to show us a weary-looking pony that they'd been sheltering from the wind. I don't know what we said, but our dumbfoundedness hung like icy breath in the air. To me, it seemed much more likely that I was dreaming or hallucinating than that this could be really happening.

The old man rambled on. "I'm glad you come out. Dunno 'bout your dog. He gonna be okay with the pony, y' think?"

"We've got the dog. But what are you *doing* here?"

"Seen your barn. Pony here needs a place t' stay. Cain't go no futher. Thought maybe you might help. You the ones with the horses, ain't you?"

"Horses?"

"Arabs?"

"Our neighbors have Arabian horses just down the road—"

"You ain't Druker then? I seen the shadow of your barn, figured—"

"Drukers are the next place down, about half a mile down on your right. Is the pony for them?"

"Nope, pony's just had it, that's all. Pregnant. That's why we're walkin' her, 'fraid she'd lose it if we tried truckin' her. Walked her here all the way up from Hammondsport. How far's that? Ten, twelve mile if it's a step. We suppose t' take her over t' Altay, but I knowed she wasn't gonna make that—so's then I remember hearin' 'bout some folks with Arabs here'bouts, figure they might least lemme put her up for the night."

"Yes, I'm sure they will," I said. No matter how outlandish his story, at least it was, more or less, of this earth.

"Well, if you'd hold onto your dog, guess we better git her goin'. 'Preciate your help."

The boy never said one word. I held Star by the collar and watched the three of them disappear back into the swirling murk of the moaning storm.

The next morning Bobbie called Helen Druker and found out that indeed they had kept the pony overnight. The man had called home for a ride back to Hammondsport. Then this morning he had come back with the boy, and they had all resumed their long walk to Altay.

· 35 ·

SMOKEY JOE

When the pony came, it was less on account of magic than of misfortune. A month or so after the night of pony strangeness, we were at Claire Tarlach's Annual After-Christmas Party, and in light conversation mentioned that we'd been thinking about getting Annie a pony. These being country people, most of them had pony stories and opinions, the consensus being that ponies were undersized, useless, stubborn, mean and that we'd be much better off getting Annie a small horse. A while later, though, a quiet woman named Glenda, a friend of Claire's whom we didn't then know, sat down next to Bobbie and said that she had a pony, a dusky old Shetland/Welsh named Smokey Joe that they'd never really had any trouble with. Her son Mike had outgrown the pony and she thought it might be just right for us. Smokey was certainly no "show" pony, she said, but he deserved a nice home. She invited us to bring Annie out, to give them a chance to get to know each other while Smokey was still on his own turf. If they got on, she'd be glad to give him to us. Though, if we also wanted the tack, she guessed maybe she'd need to get about $40 for that.

We didn't mention any of this to Annie until the weather broke. Then we all went out to Glenda's farm in Guyanoga Valley on the other side of Penn Yan. Smokey Joe was very large for a pony, in fact mulish in both size and attitude. He'd been on the same farm with the same family for fourteen or fifteen years, and Glenda thought it'd probably take four or five visits and a couple of riding lessons before he'd accept Annie enough to do what she told him. Glenda's son Mike, who was very good natured despite the fact that he was suffering from cerebral palsy, was naturally unhappy about losing Smokey, but still explained matter-of-factly that he knew that he was getting a little too big for a pony, and it was also getting a little hard for him to ride Smokey as often as he needed. Mike and Annie hit it off fine, but Mike especially loved spending time with Zack, showing him the miniature track of racing cars that he had set up in his room while Annie spent her time as close to Smokey as she could get. Later, it seemed mostly for Zack's sake when Mike hauled himself out to the pasture and showed that he could still get up on Smokey if he really tried. Glenda stood back with us, proudly and nervously watching as Mike teetered up on a couple of blocks, grabbed hold of Smokey's long dunnish mane, and struggled to pull himself up and onto the pony's back.

"It's so good for him to have a friend here to play with," Glenda said softly. "He just can't make it at school anymore. I've got him on a waiting list to get into special-ed classes. He needs so badly to have friends. I'm afraid he's going to get sick of me. I'm the one who has to nag him to do his exercises every day, and they're so painful for him that it's always a fight. Zack plays so well with him, it does my heart good, too."

After a very short time, Mike's body was hurting too much for him to stay on Smokey, and Glenda came to help him down. It was painful to think that we'd be taking his pony away from him, but Glenda seemed to have no doubts that it was for the best. Certainly, from the rough way that Mike had mounted the pony, we could clearly see that Smokey was very sturdy and patient and not the least bit mean.

Bobbie took Annie and Zack to Glenda's several more times. Glenda was so pleased for Mike to have the company that she gave Annie riding lessons as part of the mix, and it wasn't long before Smokey began trusting Annie enough to follow her lead. The next time I went to Glenda's, it was to bring Smokey home. We were met there by a peculiar old codger who transported animals for a living. While Bobbie drove ahead with Annie and Zack, I rode with the man to give him directions and the whole time he gabbed nonstop about every farm we passed, and even threw in some crazy story about his having danced once with Eleanor Roosevelt.

When we finally arrived with the truck, the rest of the family was already gathered at the barn. Smokey was a bit ruffled from the trip, but Annie calmed him with all the confidence of a character from one of her favorite horse books, then led him to his new stall. The stall was lined with fluffy straw, furnished with a salt lick and a tub of fresh water. In preparation for the pony, I had also cleaned out the old dug well next to the barn and fitted it with a new pitcher pump so that we wouldn't have to haul water all the way from the house. When Annie took Smokey out to the pasture that she'd proudly helped me refence the week before, she was grinning so hard that it looked like if she stopped, she'd burst into tears.

She had her pony at last.

· 36 ·
THE HORSE OF A DIFFERENT COLOR

I always thought of ponies as small, somewhat delicate horses, but Smokey was not that small. He was about ten hands high at the withers and about as delicate as a barrel—in human terms, something like a Bulgarian weightlifter on a basketball court: shaggy, squat and a little funny.

In contrast, horses were long-legged and gracefully elegant. (To the human eye, at least, a few extra leg inches in proportion to body makes a world of difference.) Horses had silky coats, comely manes and tails suited for violin bows. Smokey was scraggly dull, had an unkempt mane and a tail so droopy that it practically swept his stall. The horse was a movie star on opening night; the pony a pudgy boy trying on his father's tux. Charlton Heston would have been a horse, Victor Borge a pony.

In personality, horses epitomized the earnest, straightforward and predictable, while ponies were wily, stubborn and independent. I grew up thinking that ponies were for the rich, but actually ponies were very prosaic, literally down to earth; a bit brighter than horses, too.

A pony could make you laugh, but there was something essentially humorless about a horse. I often felt the same way about horse *people*, too—in the deadly serious way that their lives and conversations obsessively revolved around track and tack, horse barbers and outfits, competitions and the training ring. One might put a plume on a pony and prance him around in front of children at a circus, but no one would ever use him to pull the queen's coach, devote one's life to steeplechasing him over successions of leg-breaking log barriers and brick walls, train him to strut around in six different artificial gaits including the goose step and the Tennessee waltz.

Actually, Smokey insinuated himself into our family circle far beyond my expectations; perhaps not to the extent of our dogs and cats, but certainly more than any of the other animals. Sometimes we even felt sorry for him all by himself out in the barn, alone except for mice and rats and an occasional feral cat that was looking more for food and shelter than company. At least in the summer he had the swallows, whose constant swirl kept the lower barn O'Hare-like busy in the tending of their mud-thatched nests and precious lofty cargo.

It surprised me how social Smokey was. Annie spent time with him every day, giving him feed and water every morning and usually riding him after school, but that wasn't enough. Whenever any of us went to the barn, even in the top section—getting the lawn tractor, selecting lumber, shooting a few baskets at my Hoosier-necessary hoop—Smokey always came galloping in from the pasture to knock about his stall and whinny for attention. I usually brought him a wild apple or gave him a handful of grain, and a good scratching under the hempish macramé shag behind his ears, but even that wasn't enough. Smokey liked to be out and about, and he was amazingly persistent about getting what he liked. He liked being around the house, where the action was. He liked to help himself to the wild apples, sugar pears and numerous delights in the garden. He especially liked to trot off down the road, defeat our neighbors' electric fence, get in and prance around with their fancy Arabians. Whenever that happened, Helen Druker would call us in a panic.

"Bobbie, your pony's loose in my corral again! *Please* get him! My babies are going crazy watching him run around free out there. I'm afraid he's going to start teaching them his little tricks! Pretty soon he'll have them kicking out of their stalls. One of my babies could break a leg! And, my God, they've got to show in Palmyra on Saturday; I'll never get them braided with that pony out there!"

"I'm sorry, Helen, we'll get him—Annie's already on her way."

Our own electric fence was so ineffective at keeping Smokey in that I soon had to take it down and replace it with three tight strands of barbed wire, which was what he had been used to at Glenda's. Not only had he been willing to endure a 110-volt jolt to attain his freedom, he'd also learned how to short out the fence. The barbed wire was more effective, except that whenever the ground was soft—after a snow thaw or a good rain—from my writing window I could see him backing his rear end up against one of the fence posts and waggling the post back and forth patiently. At first I just thought he was scratching himself, but he always seemed to find the weakest post, working it steadily until it finally loosened enough for him to push it flat with a hoof or his hard head—*and he was out!*

One time he led me down the big hill and about a mile down Gravel Run Road, stopping to graze until I could almost grab him and then romping another fifty feet or so ahead of me. When I finally got hold of him I was so worn out and mad that I mounted him bareback and rode him most of the way home, despite what that did to my unstable back.

Another time, old Ann Arbor friends of ours, Roger and Katie, were visiting for the weekend. They were sleeping in the living room on our fold-out couch, in midsummer, when all the windows were open. Just before dawn we were awakened by a sudden scream, then Roger's voice yelling up at us: "HEY, HEY! HATE TO WAKE YOU GUYS, BUT THERE'S A HORSE IN THE LIVING ROOM!"

I jumped out of bed in mid-dream and stumbled my way down the shadowy dark stairs; then, coming in through a window with the earliest turquoise glow, I saw Smokey—who'd come up on the porch, pushed out the screen and was stretching his head into the house as far as he could.

I laughed. "It's not a horse, Roger—it's a pony."

· 37 ·
VISCH AND HOBBIT

Annie hardly had Smokey in hand before she started wanting a real horse. She loved Smokey, but he was terrible to ride, hard to train—impossibly intransigent. Sometimes Annie came stomping back from the barn in tears. "I'm going to murder Smokey! He won't do *anything!* I'm going to kill him!" Most of the time, though—not about to be bossed by a pony—she outstubborned him: chucking her heels into his ribs for as long as it took to get him going. If she couldn't keep him from balking, she could at least keep his bit too tight for him to get down to whatever tasty-looking tuft he'd stopped to nibble.

Sometimes, when he didn't want to be ridden at all, he took her off into the bushes and tried to rub her off, or literally tried to clothesline her—on the clothesline strung from a nail on top of the woodshed to the thriving maple tree that we'd planted when Annie was born. While he never bucked or bit or kicked, he once stomped her foot so hard that she came crying back to the house with half a hoofprint indented through her boot and into her small foot—her tears as much from anger and frustration as from pain. Nearly every day after school, Annie rode Smokey up and down the road, but when he got tired he often just turned into the driveway and sprinted for the barn. While the two of them were pretty well matched, most times Annie won by a hard nose and a stone-set jaw.

Actually, her more intractable problem with Smokey was an esthetic one: After helping Helen Druker with her Arabs, setting up the horse miniatures in her horse-postered upstairs bedroom, pouring over her *Horse & Rider* magazines, reading and rereading *Black Beauty, My Friend Flicka, The Black Stallion* and especially *Ruffian*—she'd have to diminish her elegant cantering dreams to Smokey's keg-shaped balkiness. Worst of all were the Saturday mornings when she went riding with her classmate Jenny Dean, who had a real horse and always made mocking fun of Annie trying to keep up on her stubby stubborn pony. In short—Smokey was terrible to ride, no way as beautiful as a horse, and an embarrassment to boot!

We made a deal with Annie: We'd let her get a horse when she saved up enough money to buy it, and then we'd pay for the tack and the expenses of keeping it. To help, we found extra chores to pay her for, and she also saved all the money she got for Christmas, Hanukkah and her birthday—even writing letters to the relatives to tell them of the bargain and plead for money. We still figured it would take her at least two years, and by then she'd be old enough to handle a horse and take proper care of it.

In the meantime, Jenny Dean gave Annie a pet rabbit—a huge mohair-soft black-and-white rabbit that Jenny said she didn't want anymore because it was *vicious!* I think the Deans raised rabbits both for pets and food. From what Annie said, they let the nice rabbits be pets, but if they got "mean," they were meat. Something like that. It was never quite clear to us whether Jenny was saving her pet by giving it to Annie or what was really going on, but Annie gladly took it—and named it Visch.

While I was not enthusiastic about having a pet rabbit, I dutifully helped Annie build it a cage which we made room for on the grooming table next to Smokey's ample corral-type stall. Annie insisted that she would do all the work of keeping Visch, adding that at least Visch would be a little company for Smokey until she got her horse. If she had to she would even use some of her savings for the rabbit chow. I said that I didn't think she'd have to do that.

Visch did not last very long. One morning the cage was open, and he was gone. Annie went around calling for him. I previously had been surprised to see that he would in fact come to her when she called his name. This time, however, he did not come and she eventually found him in rigor mortis out in Smokey's pasture. At first she blamed Smokey, saying that he must have stepped on Visch; but later she admitted remorsefully that, no matter how he had died, he could not have gotten out if she had latched his cage properly.

Jenny felt so sorry for Annie that she offered to give her another rabbit, and, while I was even less enthusiastic than before, the fact that she had taken responsibility for Visch's death seemed worth a second chance. The second rabbit was a calico with black on top of its feet, "Just like *Hobbit!*" Annie reminded us. And so Hobbit it was.

Annie took good care of Hobbit. A few months later, however—when we had just returned from a short vacation—Annie hurried out to see Hobbit, then came running back from the barn screaming in horror. Something—probably rats—had gnawed into Hobbit's cage and *eviscerated* him!

In sympathy, Annie's classmate friend Julie—Ed and Vera Dombroski's granddaughter—gave Annie a small enameled plaque with two bunnies on it. In red ink on the back of the plaque, Annie drew two hearts and wrote *Visch* inside one heart and *Hobbit* inside the other. Under the two hearts, in blue and green ink, she wrote: "I will look at this and remember my two rabbits. Visch—got away—found dead. I was 10. Hobbit—went on vacation, found him in cage partially eaten. I had him when I was 11."

· 38 ·

ELIJAH

It probably would've been better and kinder for us to have put Star down in the fall before, but when it comes to dealing with an old friend in precipitous decline it's not always so easy to know what "better and kinder" is. She wasn't really in any great pain. It wasn't as if she had unhealing sores crazily forcing her to tear herself to pieces. She hadn't gotten snappy and unpredictable as many old dogs do. Nor was she falling-down weak, or completely deaf or blind. Though her once-bright leonine eyes were now clouded by growing cataracts, and her once-amazing sense of hearing had so diminished that she now often jumped with a start when I came up and touched her from behind. And in a way especially common to shepherds, her hips had so degenerated that even climbing onto the porch now took a concentrated effort.

Yet, she still came out to greet us whenever we came home, her thick rope tail still beating against us despite her failing hips. She still had her teeth and a good appetite, could still reduce a beef bone to a spot of slick grass. She still always followed me into the woods, still always came with us on walks, except that now she stayed close instead of racing off after every squirrel, partridge and stray scent.

Maybe it was even a good thing for Zack and Annie to live through Star's decrepitude before having to deal with the analogous decline of aging relatives. Or maybe there wasn't anything good about it at all. In any case, that winter was very hard on her old bones. On bitter-cold days, we often brought her into the house, which—after all the years of keeping her out— now caused her to slink down guiltily, the joy of each inside moment fraught with expectations of imminent disapproval.

In early spring, while we were still harboring hopes that warmer weather might get her through one last summer, Bobbie brought up the subject of getting a puppy. We knew the kids would jump at the idea, of course, but I wasn't very enthusiastic.

Trying to soften me up, Bobbie said Star might even help train the puppy to the property lines and garden perimeters. Seeing that I found those arguments about as lame as Star was, she cut to a deeper point: Assuming we'd be getting another dog very soon after Star anyway, wasn't it going be even harder and very unfair to the puppy to just bring it home blatantly as Star's replacement?

While I had to agree with that, my heart still wasn't in it.

I tried to force myself to think of it in purely practical terms: A vital dog was a great asset in the country, but Star was hardly even any good as a doorbell anymore—let alone Queen of the Hill; terror of garden varmints; relentless sentinel against intruders, unwanted hunters or whatever else a creaky old farmhouse might bring to mind—all those things that she used to be, in additon to being the loyal friend that she *still* was. Practicality was not the real issue here!

When we went to the Bath SPCA where we'd gotten Star, Annie was dying for a husky and Zack wanted something more like a black Lab. Almost anything would've been fine with me, I just didn't want one of those dumpy little brown dogs that you see so many of out in the country, mostly called "Brownie." And I didn't want a dog that looked anything like Star—German shepherds and moose were out. Surprisingly, there were almost no puppies to choose from, a few older dogs, a pathetically lifeless litter of some poodlelike things, but nothing seemed right at all for us.

The next time, Bobbie and the children went without me and came back from the Watkins Glen shelter with a big-eyed brown male puppy. It was impossible to say what exactly was in it—beagle? Lab? spaniel? hound?—but its enormous feet suggested bigness. It went from Annie's arms to Zack's to Bobbie's, racing about as nonstop as its tail, a throbbing half-pint of energy that quickly made me feel about ten years younger, too. If my heart didn't exactly melt, it couldn't help being warmed a bit. In its ceaseless romp from one of us to the other, the puppy also included Star, who regarded it rather neutrally until the puppy jumped all over her head, whereupon she growled at it and knocked it away like an old lioness with some other lion's exuberant cub.

After squabbling to impasse over several names, I suggested "Elijah." It was Passover week, and I explained that at traditional Jewish seders a place was always set for the prophet Elijah—or as a welcoming invitation to *any* stranger who came to the door!

· 39 ·

TWO DOGS

For several weeks, we kept Elijah in a training crate that Bobbie borrowed from her friend Diane in Dundee. I was skeptical at first and disliked having a caged dog in the kitchen, but as a housebreaking device it turned out to be quite effective. The theory was that you let the dog out of the cage only to play with or to take outside for excretory relief. Because the dog preferred not to dirty its sleeping spot, it learned quickly to associate relieving itself with going outside.

Once Elijah was housebroken, we began to feed him outside, too—which required bringing Star inside so that she wouldn't eat his food. We also set up a cozy porch sleeping spot for him, a miniature version of Star's blanketed lean-to. By now Star was too dim even to be jealous. In her younger days, when friends occasionally showed up with their inside city dogs (we were a convenient stopping off point on trips from Ann Arbor or Iowa City to New York or Boston), Star's jealous territoriality sometimes extended to territorial misunderstandings between us and our guests. They weren't about to suddenly thrust their pets out in the country cold and leave them to Star's mercy. On the other hand, it was hardly fair to Star that we allow these strange canine interlopers into the very sanctuary that she was expected to guard but forbidden to enter. Sometimes when I held Star back as our visitors whisked in their pretties, I could almost feel Star's bonehead wheels clacking strategic revenge: Okay, this simpering city cousin of mine might even get to snuggle at everyone's feet on the Moroccan rug in front of the fireplace, but sooner or later the wimpy little usurper's gotta come *out!* . . .

Not that we ever would've let Star harm a guest's pet. Nor do I even think that she actually would've hurt them if left to her own. She wasn't mean, simply very insistent about her own turf—which, in a canine way of knowing things, each of these intruding dogs understood perfectly well. But because they never got the chance to properly acknowledge her turf and work it out dog-to-dog, these poor insider pets usually spent most of their visits trapped in neurotic terror, refusing to leave the house—even to take a hasty leak—until we had Star half a mile away and downwind.

Nor was this very succoring to human friendships.

"That dog of yours is a menace—at *least* you could keep it on a chain!"

"She lives here. If you just put your dog *out* with her for a while . . . "

"I almost think you'd enjoy that! Does having a bully dog make you feel bigger and stronger? Truthfully, I wouldn't *have* a dog like that!"

It did work better when the new dog was left outside with Star long enough for her to assert her dominance. Although often embarrassing for both us and our friends to watch, after a ritual amount of lording and cowering, sniffing and threatenting, chasing and humping, Star inevitably relented, thereafter allowing the intruder begrudged rights of ingress and egress, as well as bodily and psychological relief.

However, now with Elijah, Star hardly did anything. She put up with the pup as if accepting him as heir apparent, peacefully relinquishing the mantle of power according to Natural Law and the dictates of her flagging constitution. As for Elijah, just all bouncy puppy, it was hard to know how much impact or influence Star had on him beyond being another warm body to jump on and investigate.

As Star faded into late spring, Elijah came on. He didn't grow much—despite his large feet, he never got much bigger than a country mailbox, making him look very much like one of those ubiquitous "Brownies" I'd said I never wanted. He'd long since won me over, though. He was not only entirely amiable but exceptionally smart—much smarter than Star—in fact, probably the smartest animal we ever had.

Elijah was not dramatic, like Star, but he was theatrical. He trained so easily that he was like a trick dog. With surprising ease, Annie and Bobbie taught him to Play Dead, Roll Over, Dance and Speak. A natural fetcher, he would also—obsessively—bring a ball back to anyone for considerably longer than they wanted to throw it.

From the beginning, Elijah fit into the family perfectly well, but he didn't have the heart and presence of Star. He was a chaser but not a hunter; and because he was so ineffectual at catching rabbits and groundhogs, they soon disregarded him as any real danger and became serious pests in the garden.

Maybe it was because he was so smart, but for Elijah loyalty was usually secondary to comfort. Not that he wasn't always pleased to see us whenever we came home; but if he was comfortable, he didn't feel any need to rush out to greet us. Nor was he much of a guard dog; while he always barked when someone approached the house, from then on it was up to us: we were his protector, he wasn't ours.

There was no sense of power with Elijah. I used to love seeing a truckload of hunters looking back and forth from Star to each other with that what-do-we-do-now look and then chug on to some other piece of posted woods. When Elijah barked, they just told him to shuddup.

Because Elijah hated the sound of my chain saw, whenever he saw it, he stayed put and let me go off alone. I understood. Judging by the discomfort to my own ears, I could only imagine the effect on a dog's sensitive ears. Star had also always hated the chain saw. Yet, unlike Elijah, she had always come with me into the woods—lying nearby for as long as I worked, despite the ratcheting pain. When I was about to drop a tree, I usually had to chase her away to a safe distance so that there was no chance of her panicking at the foreboding *CRACK!* and running the wrong way into its unforgiving descent. Whenever I took off in the truck, she followed invariably just in case I might be stopping alongside the woods. If I went all the way down to work the bottom woods on Gravel Run, she followed the sound and always showed up a short time later.

In a way I admired Elijah for his smartness. One look at the chain saw, and he knew that I wasn't going to be paying any attention to him. He was as quick as Star was thick.

And yet, the essence of Star's thickness was her abiding loyalty. Even when she was slowed by arthritis, she came. At age twelve, when her hips started failing and she could hardly keep up with me, she still always came. At thirteen, when her hips had gotten so bad that her back legs hardly worked, she still came—*always!*

· 40 ·

DEATH OF STAR

Even as we kept hoping that Star still might improve with the coming summer, the progressing spring found us taking fewer and fewer walks because it was so disheartening to watch her struggling to keep up. One day, ambling down the road in high spring, on a day impossible not to be out into the sweet gush of new birth and rejuvenation, as we kept trying to slow our pace to Star's, her rear end suddenly failed so completely that her back legs collapsed and she slid seat first into the culvert and couldn't get herself up again. We had to use the truck to get her home, ashamed that we'd let it come to this. It was time. And we knew it had *been* time for several months at least.

As we discussed the painful options, I had a terrible impulse to buy a box of deer slugs and do the job myself. Maybe part of me even thought it the honest and manly thing to do. My friend Ransom had shot an old dog of theirs when the time had come; and, although at the time I'd said nothing, I had in fact been shocked and deeply affected—unable to decide if I thought it somehow admirable or simply callous. Now I was even more shocked to think that I was contemplating the same act myself.

Actually, though, in our case, the heart of the impulse had less to do with "honesty" or "manliness" than with Star's trembling fear of going to the vet—or even getting into the car—since we had almost never allowed her muddy hugeness in the car *except* to go to the vet. I'm not sure when this twin fear of hers first took root—possibly after her porcupine quill ordeal. In any case, riding in the car and going to the vet were the only things I knew of that Star really dreaded, which hardly made it a very "humane" combination for sending her off. Wouldn't it be better for her to die right here—sleeping peacefully in the sun while I crept quietly up behind her? Yet, the more I played the scene over in my mind, the more I knew that, even if I had the bullets, I didn't have the heart to do it.

Looking for another alternative—wondering if there

weren't a poison pill or something we could give her—we stopped in to see a vet in Watkins Glen whom we'd never gone to before—choosing this new vet, I guess, because we liked Doc McCarthy too much to want to burden him with such a sorry task. The Watkins Glen vet told us that he didn't know of any pill that was both sure and humane. Most poisons took a long time and did terrible damage before inducing death. He advised us to give her a sedative to knock her out, and then bring her in.

Wanting to make sure that we had enough to completely knock her out, we got three pills—which the vet said was more than enough to knock out an elephant! And we made an appointment to bring her in the next morning at 11:00.

That night we told the children, so they'd have their chance to say good-bye. They cried and argued with us, and we did our best to explain why it had to be done—glad, at least, that they'd have Elijah when they got home from school, when Star was gone.

The next morning, after putting Zack and Annie on the school bus dolefully and tearfully, we buried the three knockout pills in a wad of cheese and watched with both relief and dismay as Star wolfed the cheese wad down in zestful gratitude. The vet had said that she'd start getting wobbly in about twenty minutes, and in forty-five minutes she'd be completely out.

After twenty minutes, she was wobbly and confused. An hour later, however, she was *still* wobbly—and still completely conscious! We didn't know what to do! We kept checking her. At 10:00, in her confused state, she had crawled under the deck, still conscious, gazing blearily at me as I struggled woefully to drag her out. Furiously exasperated, I had steeled myself to do this and we sorely needed to get it done! Half an hour later, when she was still the same, we hauled her up into the back of the truck and took her anyway. Bobbie and I were fighting back tears shakily. Ironically, though, in her semisedated state, Star didn't seem to mind the trip at all. Constantly glancing back at her in the rearview mirror, I thought she even looked stoned, blissfully calm, her head draped peacefully over the side of the truck bed.

When we got to the veterinary clinic, the assistant told us to bring her in through the back entrance. To us, it felt as if we were just shoving her in through the trash pickup—but our emotions were such that any way of doing this would have no doubt felt equally dismal and base. We were so very lucky, after all. Neither Bobbie nor I had ever dealt so directly with the death of a family dear one before. Jason had engendered so little affection. The deaths of three of our grandparents and several aunts and uncles had either happened at a safe distance or when we were protected by remoteness and youthful resilience. But now it was our time to be responsible for the terrible details; and even though we assured each other that Star had had as good and free a life as any dog ever could have, it still punched hard into the hollow of our beings—and also felt like a terrible prelude of things to come.

We went in with her, but we didn't stay. We said our good-byes and left her alone with the vet's assistant, telling ourselves that it didn't matter. In the clinic's front office, just as I finished paying the paltry fifteen dollars required, the vet appeared, and I lashed out at him.

"You *assured* me those pills would knock her out!"

"I'm extremely surprised they didn't—"

"*More* than enough to knock out an *elephant* you said!"

"Sometimes there are variables I don't know about—that make it difficult to calculate. I'm sorry. Uh, I know this is hard."

Bumping our way back home, the tears of anger and frustration quickly enough melted to unadulterated grief. We agreed that it really wasn't fair to blame the vet. He was right, after all—there *were* incalculable variables.

At home, we were very glad that Elijah was there, even more so when Zack and Annie got home from school.

The next afternoon, on her way home from work in Elmira, Bobbie stopped by the clinic and picked up Star's ashes, in a plastic bag inside a small square cardboard box. We had planned to scatter the ashes around the farm in some kind of little ceremony. But instead, we left the box next to the fireplace between the woodpile and our old upright piano, joking morbidly that being in the house with us was where she *really* would've most wanted to be. Strangely, we left the ashes there for many months, until we finally moved the box to a shelf in the back of our old pine cupboard alongside the living-room wall, out of painful sight, but still solidly near, and we haven't found a better place for her yet.

· 41 ·

MOCHA

As soon as she had enough money saved, Annie commenced her search for the most perfect-gentle-vibrant-beautiful $600 horse in the world. Which turned out to be Mocha. A thirteen-year old, fifteen hands high, half-Arabian/half–quarter horse dun mare with a white diamond on her forehead and a dark grulla stripe running from the top of her tawny mane to the tip of her creamy silk tail. After weeks of answering ads and following word-of-mouth leads, the search finally ended at a seedy sidehill farm near the Pennsylvania border where Mocha had been lovingly owned by a woman named Candy, who also owned a high-spirited pinto and an amazing Star-sized dog that was half-husky and half–timber wolf.

Before agreeing to sell Mocha, Candy asked as many questions of us as we did about the horse, practically demanding character references before giving Mocha up. Obviously, her asking price of $650 was secondary to placing Mocha in good hands.

"She's very gentle, rides both English and Western. A perfect first horse for a young rider. My problem is that I hardly have time to ride her anymore and I'm running out of pasture for the two of them. Mostly, when I do find time to ride, it's on Paintbrush here. He's a little wild, but we're working on it. On the other hand, Mocha's pure sweetheart. All she needs is love and attention, and to be ridden a little more."

We had Mocha for three years. Once, in the first summer that we had her, she bolted unexpectedly into the woods—Annie, riding bareback, held onto her mane with both fists until she was finally knocked off by a low-hanging limb. The next day, despite her fear and bruises, Annie saddled and bridled Mocha up tearfully and rode her back over the same ground. We never knew why Mocha bolted that once, but it never happened again. While Bobbie and I were proud of Annie's grit, we understood how dangerous that romp in the woods was and how foolish we'd been not to have been more worried. Mocha was immensely more powerful than Smokey; after that, whenever Annie stretched her out to a full gallop it was almost more than we could watch. Like all parents, we were never sure how much to loosen the reins and how much to wrap them as tightly to us as a rosary or tefillin. Nothing ever tempted me to bargain with heaven as much as putting our children on the road; yet, in the long run—after all the lessons, precautions and advice—our hands held nothing but worry and hope.

In comparison to Smokey, Mocha was well-behaved and entirely unimaginative. With that one bolting exception, Mocha always predictably responded to unambiguous cues and a firm hand. She never tried to get out of the pasture on her own—getting out to follow Smokey only when he knocked down the fence. Even on those occasions, she readily returned to confinement. While she certainly relished apples, carrots and grain, she nonetheless seemed quite content with whatever we put in front of her. Unfortunately, at one point what we put in front of her was some very dusty and moldy hay, which brought on a long bout of coughing and wheezing so severe that even the farrier and the vet diagnosed her as having degenerative and incurable emphysema.

That was in the second winter that we had her. I think it was partly the sickness and presentiment of Mocha's mortality that caused Annie to begin detaching herself from Mocha, in addition to a burgeoning interest in boys and punk rock. The following fall, Annie sold Mocha to a young woman named

Tara who'd always been friendly and helpful to Annie. Tara lived in town and worked at Ken's Luncheonette. However, her fiancé's parents, the Boudinots—who were also friends of ours—owned a dairy farm and were willing to let Tara keep Mocha there—and Smokey, too. Because Mocha was now fifteen and in uncertain health, Annie only asked $250 for her—the price also mitigated by the inclusion of Smokey, the wily, crotchety twenty-six-year-old pony not exactly sweetening the deal.

· 42 ·

UGLY BILL

Ugly Bill came to die. Where he came from or why he chose our house we didn't know; but, despite the havoc that his presence created, there was something about him we couldn't refuse. He was just an old tomcat, but he felt more like the last of a species: Jack Palance in *Requiem for a Heavyweight*, Clint Eastwood in *The Unforgiven*, Toshiro Mifune in *Sanjuro*—the pugilist facing his final battle, the gunfighter putting up his guns, the worn-out warrior looking only for a quiet place and a few last peaceful days.

He was a large, burly cat, maybe not the biggest I'd ever seen but like a feline pit bull with three-quarters of his weight frontloaded into his chest, shoulders and neck—a tabby cat, like Shiver—except without any flabby, cushy middle, without any luster or powder-puff softness to his fur, and with only a nub of tail. It was hard to tell if he was a true Manx or had just lost the rest of his tail somewhere along the way. His face was scarred like an old hockey goalie's, and one of his ears had been half-chewed, too. When we first saw him, he was swaggering slowly on the wide path between the barn and house. We immediately called him "Ugly Bill."

Oddly, Elijah never even barked. Elijah and Bill, nearly the same size, were buddies from the start. Elijah was only a year old, then, and still very frisky. Occasionally, Bill indulged Elijah, wrestling and sparring lightly, but never baring his teeth or claws. Mostly, Bill just sat squarely in the sun, let Elijah romp all over him, simply shrugging him off when he'd had enough. Within a few days, the two of them were sleeping curled together in Elijah's shelter and were even eating together out of the same dish.

We never really made a decision to keep Ugly Bill, we just didn't get rid of him. At first we thought he'd stay only a few days and be on his way. Then it became more and more clear that he'd decided he was home. Bill spent a lot of his time prowling in the woods and hunting in the barn. When he came around the house, he was always friendly, often rubbing up against our legs wanting to be scratched. Sometimes, in a ratchety low voice, he even purred.

The problem was Shiver. Kitty pretty much ignored Bill, but Shiver suddenly turned violently neurotic, his whole simple-brained being overtaken by an endless nightmare of freaked-out hysteria. He refused to go outside. When Bill was near the house, he frequently began sudden fits of moaning, keening, howling as though he were being skinned alive. Tense atop one of our laps, the world's formerly most placid cat would suddenly stiffen and wail, often biting and scratching one of us in sheer terror before we could get him off us. Shiver's personality changed so radically that we even considered taking Ugly Bill to a shelter, but that seemed too cruel a way for such a valiant old warrior to die.

For two months or so, Shiver stayed inside and miserable; Bill stayed outside and implacably himself. One day, just as winter was beginning to brew, Zack came upon Bill crouched motionlessly under one of the unruly yews in front of the house—quiet, taut in the classic pose of a hunting feline. Suddenly Zack realized that he wasn't hunting or posing. Old Bill was stiff as a statue and just as dead. He had no visible wounds. Crouched like that with his neck arched and mouth agape, he looked poised for battle, as though ready to take Death on as one last challenge.

It was amazingly appropriate that Ugly Bill should be the only animal I ever saw that was dead on its feet. It was also amazing to me that, even in death, Bill commanded a respect that brooked not a whisker of pity or sentimentality. As sorry as we were to lose him, no tears were called for and none were shed, not even by Annie or Zack; we simply gathered together to bid him good-bye.

I dug a hole in the field beside our house, picked him up with my shovel and gently set him in the hole. As I did, however, the awkward top-heavy curve of his rigor mortis caused him to roll over on his back, his stiffened bent legs forced upward in a way that now made him look as if he were cringing at the sky.

"We can't bury him looking like that!" Zack said.

Everyone instantly agreed. And so I turned him over,

propped him back onto his feet and covered him over like that. Within the week, Ugly Bill had been raised to mythic status, and Shiver had returned to his old pre–Ugly Bill, insouciant self.

· 43 ·

MUTZKAH

Mutzkah arrived the same week as Super Bowl XXI(?)—the one for which Anheuser-Busch handed out free 3-D glasses as that year's inducement to get people to hold their water long enough to watch the insanely overproduced and overpriced ads. About half my softball team had come to our house, including most of the wives and a few kids. As usual, the game itself mainly stood as an anticlimactic paean to the American male's addiction to TV sports, and keg-bottom ability to decipher Roman numerals and still distinguish live action from instant replay.

On this particular day, interest had almost entirely poofed out by halftime, especially because of the unusually warm January weather, the one-sided game gratefully overshadowed by pre–Groundhog Day dreams of an early spring. Outside, the children were romping with Elijah and the two tiny white puppies that had arrived on our doorstep two days before and that we still hadn't decided what to do with.

We assumed that some irresponsible lowlife had discarded the puppies in our woods and the puppies had just followed their noses to our front porch. Of the two, one was exceptionally cute; the other not so much cute as funny-looking. Both wirehaired and mostly white, they seemed to be a mix of husky and some kind of terrier. The cuter one had the telling husky sign of one blue eye and one brown. The funny-looking one had shaggier hair, a rectangular terrier-type face and a scraggly white beard that made him look more like a model for Grand Macnish.

In fact, lately we had vaguely been discussing the possibility of getting a second dog—as company for Elijah, and in hopes of its turning out to be a more effective watchdog and garden protector than Elijah was. On the other hand, we definitely didn't want *two* more dogs! Finally we agreed that if we could find someone to take the funny-looking one, we'd keep the cuter one. To Annie, who was still dying for a husky, it was undeniable *Destiny* that this mostly-husky pup should have come right to our own doorstep!

None of my softball friends could be wheedled into taking the funny-looking pup, but two days later, when Dick Washburn came to work on our antiquated Gould water pump, he said that his daughter was looking for a puppy. The next day when he brought her over she instantly fell in love with the "cuter" puppy; and, even though we had previously explained that we were planning to keep that one for ourselves, she said that she really didn't want the other one. That night, at a serious family caucus, we decided that maybe we had misread Destiny's hand—that maybe funny-looking, unwanted beasts were best suited to our family, after all.

For a few days Annie stayed disgruntled about this not-too-subtle parental manipulation, but once the other puppy had gone she came around quickly. After all, being from the same litter, didn't both puppies have exactly the same amount of husky in them?

We called the puppy "Mutzkah," which was a Bulgarian word that Bobbie's mother used, meaning something like "the nose and mouth around one's face," as in: "Ooh, hez most adorable little *mutzkah!*"

Mutzkah remained funny-looking. He grew to be about twice Elijah's size. He was extremely affectionate and loyal, and indeed also became a terrific hunter and watchdog. He was bold and fast and, by the second summer, there was not a single groundhog or rabbit nosing around in the garden or flower beds.

Then, in the early fall of his second year, Mutzkah disappeared. For a week or so, we drove around looking for him, alerting our neighbors to watch for him, phoning "Hotline" on WFLR, and—whenever we heard or thought we heard a dog in the distance—stepping out on the porch or deck and calling loudly, over and over, howling his name out into the dry rustle of changing autumn leaves. We resigned ourselves to the fact that he was gone for good.

Nonetheless, three weeks after disappearing, on an Indian summer day when I was coming back from a wonderfully unanticipated postsummer dip in the pond, I looked up and saw Mutzkah staring down at me from the top of the pathway that led from the barn down to the pond. His weird-looking face. His long pink tongue—that always looked longer and pinker because of his whiskery flat white face—was dangling carelessly. While he seemed as happy to see me as I was to see him, there was something odd, almost apparitionlike, in the way that he just stayed there looking down at me, instead of romping down to jump all over me.

"Mutzkah, come on, boy!" I called. "Come on!"

His floppy ears perked up, but still he just stayed there. I tightened the towel around my waist and started up to meet him halfway. "You all tuckered out? You have some adventures, did you?" When he saw me coming toward him, he couldn't hold himself back any longer; but—instead of running toward me—he was only able to drag himself down the hill. His back legs were completely gone, his belly flat on the ground as his two front legs winched him forward. I quickly ran the rest of the way up the hill to curtail his struggling, dropped next to him on my knees and gave him a pitying hug, as he licked my face joyfully.

With the meagerest hopes, I took him to the new vet who had recently set up her clinic only three miles away. Maybe it was just some kind of pinched nerve or something. Maybe it was something that could be set and would eventually heal. The new vet was so softhearted that she had tears in her eyes when she told me there was nothing she could do. She couldn't tell whether he'd been shot or hit by a car or what, but there was no doubt that several of his vertebrae were crushed irreparably and his spinal cord damaged irreversibly.

Tears jumped to my eyes, too. He wasn't in any apparent pain, she said. She couldn't advise it, but she supposed he could survive for quite a few months like this. I said no, I didn't think that would be much of a kindness, and she agreed.

I held him close to me as she put the needle in one of his unfeeling back legs, thinking that, unlike old Star, Mutzkah had just been coming into his own, yet had already shown Star-like loyalty and courage—dragging himself back home to us, even though it had taken him three weeks to do it! And the best I could do was to pet him for the few seconds that it took for his trusting eyes to go blank.

· 44 ·
FUNERALS

I once drove by an Elmira pet store that had an advertisement in its front window:

THIS WEEK'S SPECIAL:
PET FUNERAL KITS — $19.99 & UP!

Even though I was driving by myself, this had me chortling all the way from Curly's Chicken House to the Clemens Center Parkway—sure that Ol' Sam Clemens himself would've snorted a chuckle at that, too. The whole thing was funny. Were people supposed to kill their pets "this week" just so they could take advantage of the "Special"? And what, I wondered, did one get for the *cheap* price—shovel, garbage bag and dog-gerel? And what with the more expensive kits—wagon, Indian bedspread and Kahlil Gibran? Or incense, dirge-on-tape and pet-shaped coffin?

I knew exactly what it took to bury a pet. Other animals, too. Both with and without ceremony—though never without a dry mouth and a few mortal pangs.

The first funeral I remembered us having was for a small chicken hawk that flew into our kitchen picture window and broke its neck. Annie was six, and she wanted us to give it a funeral. We buried it in Bobbie's large front-yard flower bed, and Annie wrote the following eulogy: "Little bird, once you were alive and now you're dead."

After that, Annie presided over a whole string of mini-funerals: birds, mice, frogs, her two rabbits Hobbit and Visch, and probably a host of other creatures that she never bothered to mention.

I also remember saying a few words over a rabid possum that I killed with a shovel under our pear tree in the backyard. It felt like the first animal that I'd ever killed so directly with my own hands, which certainly wasn't true if I considered the hundreds of flopping fish I'd beheaded, the old chicken I'd mutilated for "dinner," the hundreds of thousands of insects and spiders I'd squashed summarily—not to mention mice, bats, and countless worms. But this was somehow different, possibly because a possum is a fairly large and unusual animal. It wouldn't seem that "largeness" and "unusualness" should matter in judging a creature's individuality or worth, but it often did. And possums—despite their ugliness, their hairless ratlike tails, toothy snouts, coarse grayish hair and little pink hands—always evoked a special feeling in me because of their primitive marsupial strangeness, as though they'd somehow outlived their own longevity, beaten back both vengeful gods and evolutionary odds—all possibly due to their most famous and amazingly effective adaptation, their proclivity for *playing* dead—thereby fooling not only predators but perhaps even the Evolutionary Fates!

However, this particular rabid possum was not playing—at least, I didn't think so. I looked at it from several angles, nudged it with my shovel and turned it over. It certainly looked dead, but then if a possum's playacting was good enough to fool its natural predators, how could I be so sure? Before approaching it closer, I gave it two more awful skull-cracking whacks with my shovel. I knew that killing a rabid animal was absolutely the right and necessary thing to do. Hardly a month went by that one one of the local papers didn't run a story about some pet or person being attacked by a rabid raccoon or bat or possum or fox. Still, I felt badly about it. I dug a hole right there to bury it under the pear tree, deep enough so that Star wouldn't get it. And, as I dug, I vaguely mumbled something to make me feel better about it.

Eventually, when their times came, we buried Kitty Coffman and Shiver, each with great sadness but very few words. Fortunately, by the time we had to put Kitty down, Zack was at SUNY Binghamton—she'd always been so much more his cat than Annie's. And by the time we had to put Shiver down—always Annie's favorite—she was in her first year at Yale. It was Bobbie and I who buried the two cats, and then planted trees on their graves.

Our ritual of planting trees on graves had started with Mutzkah. After he dragged himself home so valiantly and I'd so painfully hurried him to the vet. I was all but certain that the kids would come back from school, Bobbie from work, and all I'd be able to tell them was that Mutzkah had come home, after all, but now was dead—with their never even having had a chance to say good-bye. Yet, it clearly would've been heartless for me to let him suffer until the next day just so that everyone could see the light in his funny blue eyes one more time. So I'd done the dutiful thing. And when everyone got home, we held a brief ceremony. I had a hole already dug, Mutzkah bagged and waiting in the wheelbarrow, and a tiny oak tree ready to plant over him in the hopes that it might at least be enriched by his bones and flesh if not actually by his spirit.

Later we would also plant trees in memory of Bobbie's mother, and my Aunt Florence, and Bobbie's father, and my father—for Bobbie's father a blue spruce; for Florence an ornamental pear; and for Bobbie's mother and my father—tiny saplings that had sprouted around a maple tree that Vera and Sim had planted when Annie was born, that was now ten feet higher than the peak of our barn.

· 45 ·

THREE BEARS (MYTH, JOKE AND MORAL LESSON)

We had many animals on our land whose lives seemed to run parallel to ours, so that we rarely (or never) came across them.

Our presence, of course, was unequivocally known to them—us, our carnivorous pets, our terrorizing machines—from their viewpoint, survival itself often depended on keeping a well-hidden eye on us. In fact, some of these creatures kept so well hidden that our knowledge of them was almost entirely restricted to conjecture, deduction and rumor.

From Star's mouthful of quills, for instance, we deduced the presence of at least one porcupine.

From the distinctive garbly-clacking in the woods, we knew we had wild turkeys long before we ever saw one.

Once, looking down from my writing window, I saw a weasel in our large autumn woodpile, undoubtedly looking for the mice and chipmunks whose nests and seed larders I often found tucked into and under the seasoning stack. For much of a whole day, I watched it pouring itself into spaces and bubbling up out of cracks as it looked to catch some rodent at home. While that was the only weasel in the wild I ever saw, it seemed reasonable to suppose that there were other weasels around, too. And why not a mink or a ferret?

Recently, rising out of Crystal Valley, we heard a strange lonesome howling that we were quite sure was a coyote.

Ed Dombroski used to swear that he'd once seen a bobcat behind the barn.

Hardly a year went by that someone didn't claim to have seen a bear. And while it was always very tempting to believe them, we also knew that sometimes people saw what they wanted to see.

One April Fool's Day I hauled Bobbie out of bed, rushed her downstairs, saying I could hardly believe it, but there was *moose* in our front yard! *"Where? Where?"* she cried out, so excited that—for an instant—she actually thought she saw it, antlers and all—before catching my prankster's grin and slugging me in the ribs.

And I'd always thought that the bear sightings in our area were quite a bit like that moose.

Since then, however—though not actually on our land— we have had three real encounters with bears. The first was less "an encounter" than a prickling of possibilities. The Elmira *Star-*

Gazette had a front-page story and picture of a bear that had been treed near downtown Elmira. For fear of what the panicky bear might do, state troopers were forced to shoot it, the article said. Apparently this hapless bear had wandered up from the hills of nearby Pennsylvania, where bears were said to be fairly common. And—as Elmira was only 35 miles from us—it had suddenly seemed quite possible that we might indeed have a bear in our woods, too.

Several years later, on a steamy night in mid-July, I was with two of my softball buddies strolling down Elm Street in Penn Yan, rehashing our victory or loss and heading for the Red Rooster to celebrate or console ourselves, when an untrustworthy player from a rival team yelled to us that there was a bear down by Tom's Super Duper. Mostly expecting to be superduped, we hurried over, nonetheless. Sure enough, huddled there beside the food market's Dumpster, a smallish black bear was looking very timid and confused. Within minutes, someone from the Cornell Agricultural Extention arrived with a tranquilizer gun and proceeded to knock the bear out, drag it into a cage, and remove it to whereabouts unknown.

Penn Yan being just 14 miles from us, the possiblity of our having a bear on our land had suddenly become even more excitingly real. After that, we'd several times found unidentifiable scat and large unknown tracks, but, despite speculating on their bearish qualities, we had still not seen a bear.

Our third bear encounter came when we were camping on vacation in Rimouski Park, up the St. Lawrence River from Quebec City. When we entered this wonderfully ignored wilderness preserve, I asked the ranger whether we needed to worry about bears, and he just laughed.

"Sometimes dey come into de camps. Keep your foods put away, and out of your tents, *naturellement*. If one bother you, just whistle—it probably go away. If we get too many complainings on one, we catch it and den move it to de other side of de park."

That night a very large black bear came into our camp: rummaging through our supplies and trash; climbing on top of our picnic table—even nosing up to the flimsy mesh of our tent window where we had been watching it like a hutch of bunnies watching a weasel! We whistled! We yelled and sang *"Frère Jacques!"* We banged flashlights against our canteen and Coleman lantern! But we might as well have been playing some Spike Jones relic from somewhere over in New Brunswick. When he was good and ready, the bear swaggered out of camp. And a few minutes later, we could hear him banging around in the next camp, a quarter-mile or so down the trail.

In the way that parents often feel they have to be, the next morning on our way out of the park, the three bear stories coalesced for me into an object lesson that I shared meaningfully with Zack and Annie. In the city of Elmira, where people had lost their familiarity with large animals, it had seemed necessary to kill the bear. In the farm town of Penn Yan, where people were more used to handling big animals, removing the bear had been sufficient. In Rimouski, where the warden knew the bears personally, giving them room was all that was required; they were simply a part of the shared territory.

"Well, isn't there food for thought in that?" I asked, getting no response.

"Look, in the middle of the road—there's a *moose!*" Bobbie shouted.

And when I looked, there was—the scraggliest, homeliest, most moth-eaten antlerless moose I'd ever seen, but a sure-enough, nonimaginary moose nonetheless.

· 46 ·

THE ENDS OF EDEN

As the pond began to age, maintenance became an ever-expanding problem. The few nice cattails that we had allowed to grow at both shallow ends of the dike had now grown into uncontrollable thickets spreading out and propagating by land, sea and air: their familar brown-tipped wands exploding into fluffy airborne seeds; their underwater sepals giving rise to new tender shoots; their deep-seated rhizome roots grabbing ever-more bottomland for their own. For every willow tree that I lopped, a hundred shoots came up all along its still-viable rootline. Similarly, the various strains of algae and pond grass became more entrenched each year.

Half of my "swimming" time was now taken up weeding a clear route to the open center of the pond, the only part of the pond not thick with masses of vegetation. Worse yet were the weekly hours spent arduously uprooting and discarding cattails from the muck shallows, where the *leeches* lived.

Fortunately, the leeches were small, toenail-clipping size, easy to brush off and squish before any serious attachment could take hold. Because they inhabited only the soft edges of the pond and needed some time to corner their host and cling, they weren't really a problem with swimming as long as one went off the pier or waded in quickly.

Not a problem *theoretically*. In actuality, the *idea* of swimming with leeches was so repulsive that Bobbie and the kids had stopped going into the pond altogether, even on the most sweltering summer days. We obtained a booklet on "pond leeches" from Cornell Extension, which said basically that the only way to get rid of them was by draining the pond in late autumn and letting them freeze; but we certainly didn't want to do that. While swimming in the pond had always been a great luxury, the pond was more important to us as a living aquatic habitat, an attractor of wildlife, and in each season an entity of ever-changing beauty. I didn't keep at the pond weeding as much for the sake of swimming and fishing as to sustain the pond's viablity. I wasn't sure what would happen if we just let it go, but I was afraid it would deteriorate from pond to swamp to sloggy marsh—and eventually disappear altogether.

Of course, "eventually" was entirely out of our control, but I still thought of the pond as something that we had brought into being. I still loved it and didn't want to let it disappear on our watch.

One day, while I was working waist-high in the water, in the thickest, most recalcitrant area of cattails, I picked up two much larger leeches, well over an inch long, darker and thicker than the others, one on my thigh and the other under the waistband of my swimsuit. As usual, a few of the smaller regular variety were on my feet and ankles, but these two bigger ones did not merely disgust me, they horrified me; especially when—after pulling them off—the tiny wounds they'd inflicted continued to stream blood. I finally had to varnish them shut with a styptic pencil. This, of course, was the result of their famous anticoagulant, the substance in their saliva that kept their victims bleeding freely to facilitate their liquid feast, the same property so commonly used by early "physicians" to bleed "bad humours" from their patients.

In fact, some modern doctors had again begun using leeches to keep blood from clotting during surgery. I told Bobbie that maybe we could turn the pond into a *leech farm*. She almost laughed. And I also pretty much lost my sense of humor when the leech wound on my abdomen became infected so badly that I had to have it lanced.

Shortly after that, I bought a pair of waders to wear when I worked in the pond, but, even so, I had now come to dread this work that had once been satisfying.

The History of Medicine notwithstanding, leeches to me were like the stone that God had made that was too big for Him to lift. Inasmuch as I had created this space that they now inhabited, they had now taken it out of my hands and made a mess of it that was beyond my control. In fact, if I'd been a religious person, I'd have wondered why God created leeches in the first place. Were there leeches in Eden? Bloodsuckers in Paradise? For that matter, what did *any* carnivores eat in Eden? As hard as it was to imagine lions and lambs lying side by side, wasn't it even harder to imagine them eating veggies together, lions and lambs and leeches all grazing peaceably side by side in the meadows of Eden?

· 47 ·

GRASS CARP

Grass carp (*Ctenopharyngodon idella*) are members of the goldfish family, native to the rivers of China and eastern Russia. We purchased three 8-ounce grass carp through the Yates County Office of Soil & Water Conservation . . . at $21 a fish.

Members of the *gold*fish family, all right! SIXTY-THREE DOLLARS FOR THREE LITTLE FISH THAT COULDN'T EVEN REPRODUCE. It wasn't like they excreted bullion. However, what grass carp *would* supposedly do was glut themselves up to 25 or 30 pounds. by sucking down humongous amounts of freshwater *weeds*.

To buy them, we had to have our pond officially approved and obtain a New York State Grass Carp License. These particular fish (the only grass carp it was legal to have in New York State) had been raised from eggs that had been shocked by sudden temperature extremes, changing them from fertile diploid eggs to infertile triploids, this to ensure that they wouldn't become an established species in our lakes and rivers and upset the native life balance in those habitats.

Ponds were different. Unlike long-evolved, delicately balanced natural habitats, ponds were artificially created and managed environments from the outset, and we were simply introducing one more artificial factor—like rearranging annuals and perennials in a garden, *molding* nature for our uses— the quintessentially human thing to do.

When the grass carp arrived, they came with very specific

instructions: the temperature of the pond had to be between 40 and 70 degrees; it was necessary to slowly mix our pond water in with the water the fish had been transported in; only then could they very gently be released into three- or four-inch-deep water and allowed to enter the pond.

We followed the instructions impeccably, but no sooner had the three grass carp undulated their way into the pond than there commenced a tremendous roiling of the waters. From all over the pond, our largemouth bass surged to the spot of entry, and for several minutes we watched the sickening swirl, until the water had once again returned to its usual serene state—whereupon we never again saw head or tail of any of the grass carp.

· 48 ·
MR. PHEASANT

When we first moved to the farm, someone told us that Department of Conservation had tried several times to introduce pheasants on the hill, but the pheasants didn't like it this high up and had all gone down into the valley—where, in fact, we often saw them scooting across the road or sailing brilliantly in front of our vehicles like shots being fired across our bows.

But then, local sage analysis notwithstanding, we started seeing them up top, too. By our second or third year, their urgent crowing became a common sound in the nearby fields, and it wasn't unusual for us to see one on the dike or around the barn. Mostly we saw the gorgeously plumed, ring-necked males, but once in a while we also saw a clutch of hens and chicks who were camouflaged so well that they could step into the brush and disappear before our eyes.

Pheasants are not reclusive birds, but they are understandably wary of humans, whose main reason for bringing them from China to the New World was to shoot them. We call them "game" birds, but of course they take it rather more seriously than that. Which is why it so surprised us to see a pheasant at our front-yard bird feeder. First, we saw him thirty yards or so down the road, working his way slowly up the shoulder in the direction of the house. It was winter and we thought he was probably eating beads of rock salt, or maybe gravel for his gizzard. As we watched, though, he not only came near the house, but then ducked through the thicket behind our plum tree and came right into the yard, and then up to the feeder, where he proceeded to pick up spilled seeds, along with the bluejays, cardinals and other regulars.

Our ringside excitement was generated both by his exotic beauty and by the sense of anomaly. We thought we were seeing a one-time event. Two days later, however, he was back again. And then he began coming every day. We called him "Mr. Pheasant." It seemed only right to name him because of his unusual and distinctive behavior, and because he was the boldest pheasant we'd ever seen.

A few years earlier, I'd had something of a revelation while watching a flock of goldfinches at the niger-thistle feeder on our anemic birch tree. In spring, we always loved watching their winter plumage turn progressively from dull green to bright yellow, almost as a color-coded harbinger of the returning summer sun; however, that was not the revelation. The revelation was that the previous year there had been one bluebird flying with the flock of goldfinches at our feeder, and this particular spring, when the finches reappeared, the bluebird was still with them.

And it hit me: this was not just a bluebird in a flock of goldfinches, this was the *same* bluebird in the *same* flock of goldfinches.

It almost seemed too obvious to be called a "revelation"; but for me, in my citified ways, I had mostly tended to generalize the birds. Maybe not our pear tree's two upside-down-walking nuthatches, or our lone red-bellied woodpecker (a female), or the swallows that came back to the barn every spring to reclaim their same nests. But I hadn't really thought about it. Birds seemed to come and go so freely that they seemed almost random and generic. It hadn't occurred to me that many of the same individual birds returned to us—not only day after day, but year after year.

And if something happened to our one red-bellied woodpecker, or our two nuthatches, or our eight chickadees or our particular flock of sparrows—or if they simply chose to go somewhere else—there was no surety at all that others of their kind would ever take their place. The bluebird had made me see all the birds differently.

Yet, even knowing this, I also realized that, to some degree, I couldn't help but generalize the sparrows and chickadees and cardinals because I couldn't distinguish them. Nonetheless, the upshot of this revelation was that I now presumed their individuality as well, which made me feel more closely connected and warmly disposed toward them.

I was still refining the nuances of this "revelation" when, one morning, I came downstairs and at the bird feeder saw *two* pheasants, indistinguishable one from the other. In one way it was wonderful to see two of them, but mostly I felt as if I'd lost a friend. They couldn't *both* be "Mr. Pheasant." And within a couple of weeks, a *third* pheasant appeared. And then a *fourth*.

This was like the "bluebird revelation" in reverse. Suddenly I realized that Mr. Pheasant may not have ever been one individual bird. Every day that we thought we were seeing the same pheasant, we might have been looking at some other pheasant we'd never seen before—there might have been as many different "Mr. Pheasants" as days we had seen "him." Of course it was not the fault of the pheasants, which, indeed, were all individual birds, despite my inability to differentiate them—despite my specious reasoning and the ironic contorting of my "revelation."

Nonetheless, my feelings had changed abruptly. Not only had "Mr. Pheasant" suddenly ceased to exist, but his personal history and my affection for him had become equally ethereal. And now when I looked out at the four indistinguishable birds, for a moment they made me think of nothing but a flock of fancy chickens.

· 49 ·

THE POOPHEADS

I suppose if they were the only birds we had, the cowbirds would have been among our most precious companions. We couldn't have a world without birds. Surely, more than anything else, birds embody our dreams, keep alive our ideas of lightness and song, prove the possibility of transcending all downcast weights of unlikely circumstance. Our place for heaven is in the sky. We put wings on our angels and feathers in our hats. At our happiest we say we're flying; when most inspired we say our spirits sing and soar—like birds.

Cowbirds, though, were about as uncolorful and unsavory as birds got. Rackety, unattractive, noisome. Largish birds with shiny umber bodies, dull light-brown heads and bad reputations, they built their nests in our eaves' troughs and between loose boards in our siding, their messy droppings dribbling down the sides of the house. Somewhere I read that one of their evening songs was mellifluous, but if so we were never able to identify it. The only sounds we ever associated with them were the squawking, cackling and wing-flapping that greeted us each day at the crack of dawn for as long as they were in our walls.

When we looked in our *Audubon Guide*—for some silver lining to ameliorate these thunderheads—we instead discovered that cowbirds lay their eggs in the nests of other smaller songbirds, whereupon the larger baby cowbirds push all the other eggs and baby birds out of the invaded nest so that the confused "parents" will tend only them.

More than once in late spring, when the cowbirds came back, I was tempted to get out Zack's pellet gun and pick a few of them off, hoping that the rest would take the unwelcoming hint and take their harpy ways to someone else's eaves and soffits.

Still, as dislikable as they were, killing them seemed an extreme response to mere annoyance and a little birdshit on the side of the house. So, we just renewed our efforts at finding out where they were getting in and tried to close off their access, which usually worked for a while, and, at the very least, tightened up the house a bit.

And instead of shooting them, we resorted to name-calling.

We called them "The Poopheads."

Mr. and Mrs. Poophead and all the little Poopheads!

Which Zack and Annie loved, of course. Not only giving them a legitimate excuse to use the word "poop," but also great joy in having parents who had joined the ranks of the puerile underground.

Amazingly, making a joke of them almost completely disarmed our built-up feelings of aggression. If calling them "The Poopheads" didn't exactly endear them to us, it did allow us to tolerate their company.

· 50 ·

AT THE FEEDERS

As the years passed, birds became increasingly important to us. Zack and Annie became too busy with school and friends to care about what was living in the barn. So neither did we. Although we still occasionally took beautiful walks around the pond, the weeds and leeches had made it so unpleasant that we seldom fished or swam in it anymore. And the closer that Zack and Annie came to going out on their own—and the more fragile our own parents became—the more obsessively we seemed to feel affinity with the birds. Part of it was just physical: the quick shot of color, the constant musical backdrop, the immediate way that they inevitably lifted our spirits with their quick-hearted activity. And part of it had to do with an easing of relationships—our connection to the birds was symbiotic and always tenuous: We had no "owner's" responsibility toward them. Because we fed them, they voluntarily brought their wild freedom onto the stage outside our proscenium window. And from the wings brought with them a certain inherent mid-life message: nature telling us to loosen the moorings, lighten up, give more attention to airier things.

In our efforts to attract more birds and create better vantages for observing them, our front-yard feeders went through numerous configurations, but the most common variation was this: a large hanging feeder on the mother pear tree; a second large feeder right outside our tri-part kitchen casement window—atop the three-foot-high hollow stump that we used to cover the unsightly well casing; a slender supposedly squirrel-proof tube feeder hanging on our never-healthy and now-dead birch tree; and a freestanding metal space-needle thing that accommodated only small birds, closing off the feed dispenser automatically if heavier birds or squirrels perched on it.

As our bird-craziness increased, we started to go through something like a half a ton of birdseed a year, but the effect of this arrangement made for spectacular birdwatching. All year round, but especially in the winter, the front yard was a magical whirl of birds coming and going between the woods and the trees in our yard, and from feeder to feeder.

They came singly, in pairs, in small groups, in flocks. Some came every day, others every once in a while, some only rarely—a few we saw only once (mainly during spring and fall migrations).

Once: a pileated woodpecker, a Baltimore oriole, a veery, a scarlet tanager, a redheaded woodpecker, a yellow-bellied sapsucker, a brown thrasher, a flock of red-breasted grosbeaks.

Rarely: rufous-sided towhees, a red-bellied woodpecker, eastern bluebirds, indigo buntings, flocks (the same flock?) of cedar waxwings.

Commonly: hairy woodpeckers, downy woodpeckers, yellow-shafted flickers, catbirds, evening grosbeaks, redpolls, juncos, crows, starlings, red finches, tufted titmice.

Ubiquitously: in season—redwing blackbirds, robins, fly-catchers; year round—cardinals, bluejays, chickadees, mourning doves, cowbirds, nuthatches, goldfinches, sparrows galore.

When a bird we'd never seen before came to the feeder, it was always an event, like found treasure, a piece of marvelous luck that made the world seem both larger and smaller, more mysterious and more personal. With the scarlet tanager and Baltimore oriole, it was only a matter of a few moments and gone. If they hadn't been recognizeable so immediately, we might never have noticed them. The veery, brown thrasher, redheaded woodpecker, yellow-bellied sapsucker, and red-breasted grosbeaks hung around and chowed down for several hours before moving on.

Our female red-bellied woodpecker stayed for the entire winter.

The pheasants came to the feeder only for a month or two.

(We've seen partridges on the road, but so far never in the pear tree.)

On Bobbie's fiftieth birthday, we came downstairs and saw three wild turkeys at the feeder, the only time we'd ever seen a wild turkey close to the house. That begged a few insult-added-to-injury jokes—our overriding response to the mind-tickling strangeness of it. Had we been animistic—as most of the human inhabitants on this same ground had surely been—we would've needed a shaman to help decipher the deeper significance—possibly changing Bobbie's name to Old Three Turkey. Something like that.

· 51 ·
SWALLOWS AND CHICKADEES

The swallows and chickadees have always been special to us. On the one hand, they're clearly wild; but on the other, they exist in such proximity to us that they seem almost like friends. Of all the creatures around us, they alone fill this particular niche. One of the reasons is that, of all the birds, they are also the boldest.

Chickadees often remind me of Dickensian street urchins, little pickpockets. Their black-and-white faces even make them look like they're wearing masks. While the other birds wait until we fill the feeders and move out of range, the chickadees take advantage of their absence and zip in, even dipping into the feed bucket itself or flying into the bottom of a 50-lb. feedbag while our hands are still in it. The chickadees are always first in line. After a car or truck rattles by on our rough dirt road, sending all the birds scattering into the trees, it's always the chickadees who come back first. Even when the jays and cardinals and grosbeaks are running sorties at each other and jousting for dominance, a chickadee will fly in right between them like a bantamweight referee pushing apart a couple of fuming heavyweights. *"Excuse me, I'll take that little white millet seed right there—okay, resume fighting, I'm outa here."*

Recently we had a sharp-shinned hawk come to the feeder—not for the little seeds but for the little birds! With its slate gray suit and buff brocaded vest, clear creamy markings and fluffy white leggings, it was an extremely handsome accipiter—except maybe for its glistening talons and the hungry "repo man" look in its ruby eyes. Perched insolently on the feeder closest to the window, its head kept swiveling, like an evil dictator looking for someone to behead. Except that there were no other birds to be seen; none that wanted to be within half a mile of this fellow. Until suddenly the chickadees began to reappear: first one or two in the plum tree, then to the pear tree; suddenly five or six of them, one after another, bopping happily from feeder to feeder like Charlie Chaplin tramps left all alone at a banquet buffet. The hawk glared at them a few times; then—knowing it couldn't catch them—took off, as though unable to endure their cheeky hubris any longer.

Once I was walking along the farthest boundary of our land, a place where I very seldom go, following deer trails and an empty creek bed through the thorny brambles and thick-wooded hedgerows. Suddenly I heard the *dee dee dee* of a chickadee and stopped. Because we were so used to chickadees being around the house, it surprised me to find one in the wild.

Then I heard another *dee dee dee* behind me. Then also to my left and to my right. Pretty soon there were eight or ten of them in all, all buzzing me with their *dee dee dee*, flying in closer and closer to me until I was strangely surrounded. I tried to talk to them and coax them to my outstretched hands, but I must have been near their nesting area and they were having none of that. They were defiantly letting me know that I was too close to something of theirs, and our "friendship" out here was very much in question. I cheeped back at them for a few moments, then acceded to their pleas and lumbered on.

Occasionally, Bobbie has been patient enough to get a chickadee to land on her outstretched hand and eat from her palm—one seed at a time. Chickadees always take one seed at a time, fly away with it to a nearby perch, eat it there, then come back for one seed more—and off again. It hardly seems that a single tiny seed can produce enough energy to support all that flying and taking off, but chickadees are among the most energetic and tireless of birds—so quick that, as we used to say, they can cut on a dime and leave you nine cents change.

Swallows are bold in a different way. If chickadees are Artful Dodgers, then swallows are little Zorros. Their flat black heads like Spanish hats, their wings cut like black cloaks, their flying style the flourish and thrust of rapiers and foils. Swallows wouldn't be caught dead at a bird feeder or eating from a proffered hand. They fend strictly for themselves, living very nicely by taking insects on the wing. I don't know why they choose to live in such proximity to humans. Maybe it's because they know that humans attract a lot of insects, and humans also offer suitably protective shelters for their sturdy adobelike nests. Porches and basement barn joists are perfect for their purpose.

Often when I'm mowing the lawn, swallows swirl around over my head, feasting on the insects that fly up to escape my whirring blades. Very social among themselves, they jabber constantly to one another, even in flight. They also like to line up ten or twelve in a row on the peak of a roof or on an electric wire. They don't so much sing as talk to one another. Or it seems like talking, because of the large variety of clicks, clucks, chirps and buzzing that sound like across-the-street gossip or an audience just before curtain time. Sometimes I can't resist joining in, trying to imitate some of their noisy chatter, though I've yet to have one give me as much as a sideways look in response.

The swallows are very dear to us for a number of reasons, more than for the magnificence of their zigzag flight, the enormous numbers of mosquitoes and biting flies they eat, the animation they give to the lonely depths of the old barn. For us they also have symbolic significance. When the swallows return, it's almost as if they validate the fact of spring, as if spring is no longer in the process of "coming," but is here to stay. In late April, two or three "scouts" appear first, for half a day or so reconnoitering, I suppose to make sure that their nests are still in place. With tremendous soaring, swerving verve they arrive, zooming in and out of the barn, over the pond, over their territory back and forth, yapping all the while. Then, a day or two later, the rest of the flock follows, twenty or thirty strong.

For nine straight years (and maybe more before we made the connection), the swallows returned on April 26, our wedding anniversary, which always seemed like a special gift. In fact, their punctuality on that date had started to seem almost eerie—until one year when they didn't make it until April 28.

Once when we were vacationing in the Yucatán, we met up with our swallows in the winter home. They probably weren't *our* swallows, of course, but we had read that many of the swallows wintered in Mexico, and their behavior was so much the same that it was like seeing our old friends in their other lives: swirling over the arid fields, swooping to take insects over the Gulf of Mexico. I wondered if they lived in the makeshift barn shelters that we saw, where the burros and scrawny Mexican cows were kept. I wondered whether, every October, some Mexican farmer eagerly awaited their return, perhaps as a sure sign that the broiling summer had finally abated for good.

And when they left in April, did he wish them safe journey, wonder about their summer abode, and perhaps even wonder about his *norteamericano* counterpart who was watching for their return?

· 52 ·

BLUEJAYS AND CARDINALS

Bluejays and cardinals capture the eye, especially in midwinter, when spirits tend to white out in the bland sameness and lack of color. The flash of a bluejay is like a flag of hope, soul-soothing as crested waves rolling on a beach. A cardinal—within the sketchy branches of our pear tree against the virgin snow—at various times reminds one of a heart in a rib cage, a haiku, a Mount Fuji silkscreen, a scene in Chinese porcelain.

About half the time our bluejays and cardinals come to the feeders together, sometimes only two or three, but other times as many as twelve or fourteen of each, a glorious feast of color— such a blur of scarlet and blue that they become impossible to count—sometimes all crowding into the pear tree at the same time, making it look like a Christmas tree with living ornaments.

I grew up believing that cardinals were "good" and bluejays "nasty." We were taught that. I still hear it. But I've come to think that bluejays have gotten a bad rap, most likely based purely on appearances and our human need to pose such dualities. Against the blank slate of winter, cardinals and bluejays are the two most unignorable entities and thereby are objects naturally paired for comparison:

Cardinals are the color of blood, vitality, sanguinity and passion. Bluejays the icy indifferent color of sea and sky.

The calls of a cardinal are sonorous and musical, while a bluejay's voice is more like a metal spoon scraping the bottom of a pan.

Cardinals are clearly identifiable as male and female, which helps us to anthropomorphize them into cozy couples and courting lovers. But because bluejay gender is more difficult to distinguish, we tend to see them more as mechanically sexless and androgynous.

Cardinals appear well-groomed, their modest well-shaped beaks descending in a straight line from their comely crests. Bluejays are ganglier—often seeming unkempt and scraggly— with wickedly stilettolike beaks jutting straight out as though ready to thrust home.

But are the *behaviors* of the two really that different?

If cardinals and bluejays don't exactly flock together, they certainly move in similar circles; it's rare for us to have one at the feeder and not the other. Both aggressively displace smaller birds at the feeders, as well as members of their own kind. After a brief nosh, birds of each typically move to a nearby branch, or interact directly with their own—chasing, squabbling, preening, calling—bluejays *always* with other bluejays and cardinals with other cardinals; within each species: males get in each other's faces, males chase females, solitary birds in treetops call back and forth, bunches fly off together by themselves or with others of their kind in mixed flocks.

Between species: while there's a constant flow of bluff aggression and posturing, I've never seen a bluejay actually attack any kind of bird—except another bluejay. Which is also true of cardinals, and of all the other bird species at the feeders—large, small, gaudy bright, or dirt plain. All vie for position and push in for whatever they can get, but never—in the constant fussing and strafing—did I ever see any bird at our feeders actually do damage to another bird. Rather, our feeder birds all seem part of the same grand interspecies dance buffet: a little random pushing at the food table, the strutting, preening, fighting and chasing strictly for the sake of their *own* kind.

· 53 ·
MR. CARDINAL

We didn't know it at the time but there was a dark foreboding in the odd behavior of an obnoxious male cowbird which was, for some days, fixated frequently on his own image in our tri-part kitchen casement window—fifteen or twenty minutes at a crack perching on the low branch of a hackberry, glaring at the reflection of his own most threatening and terrifying visage: neck bowed, eyes piercing, greasy black feathers ruffed and flashing—all the while emitting his shrill liquidy-glottal, umlautlike war cry: *Schueureee! Schueureee!*—then *thwap!*—flying at the window to attack his ghostly "rival" in the glass!

Over and over. *Schueureee, thwap! Schueureee, thwap!* Thirty or forty blitzkrieg forays per session before finally withdrawing from the field of honor to regather his marbles, machismo—or whatever birds have instead of testosterone.

Half a day of this, and I was on the verge of losing it, too.

At one point, suddenly noticing that his pecking had marred a section of the window about the color and size of a muddy heelprint, I went outside to inspect, afraid he'd damaged the glass permanently. The marring, however, was merely an accumulation of beak-slobber excretion, which a dab of Window-Plus took right off.

At first, that's what saved Mr. Poophead. Had he ruined our double-insulated Andersen Perma-pane—especially given my predisposed antipathy toward poopheads in general, my rising annoyance at this poophead in particular, my own territorial instincts—but the window was still intact. For a while there was even something fascinating in trying to fathom his strange compulsion.

As the days wore on, however, the more maddening this behavior became. I began thinking that maybe *this* was what had driven Edgar Allan Poe off his rocker—rap-rap-rapping at his chamber door until he began imagining bodies in the walls with hearts that wouldn't stop beating.

As I more and more began thinking of blasting the fool thing to hell, I was surprised and even embarrassed by the thinness and fragility of my "tolerance" veneer.

How easily violence could raise *its* ugly head and start rapping.

During the several days that Mr. Poophead's quixotic behavior continued, I think what really saved him was that sanguinary reflection I kept seeing on *my* side of the glass. Then finally he stopped. Had he finally knocked some sense into himself? Succumbed to self-inflicted brain hemorrhage? Surrendered the coveted spot to his "apparition self"? Fallen dizzy prey to hawk talons? Or perhaps the poophead mating/nesting/*mano a mano* season had simply ended.

Whatever the reason, the annoying poophead episode was over—except as a foreboding precursor to Mr. Cardinal.

Later that spring when a male cardinal assumed the same position that Mr. Poophead had relinquished only a month or so before, the situation took on an entirely different meaning— far beyond the mystery of why these two episodes should have stepped on each other's heels in such a strange way. Nevertheless, one after another, these two birds played this same bizarre springtime scene—a scene that we'd never seen before or since.

It was almost as if the cardinal was the cowbird's understudy. Or was there something unique in that year's light? Or some essence of insanity in the air exuded by some rare-blooming and oddly intoxicating plant? Why, in some years, did countries all over the world go crazy and similarly conclude the necessity for war? It was that kind of thing. It defied any kind of sense, but there it was.

Mr. Cardinal, however, significantly escalated both his neurotic symptoms and our emotional stakes. Unlike the lowly cowbirds, cardinals to me had always been something like sacred hearts in the mother's bosom. Going back to my earliest days, that's what I first crayoned in art class: cardinals in the winter, robins in the spring. The cardinal was the Indiana state bird, its picture over the blackboard in the corner above the state and national flags, in the same row as the pictures of George Washington, Abe Lincoln and President Dwight D. Eisenhower.

If I refused to buy into the "nastiness" of bluejays, I had never doubted the inherent goodness and beauty of cardinals. There was a residue in me that still thought it a crime and a sin even to think of harming a cardinal. That was the loftiness that cardinals still had in my subliminal estimation, and how far a cardinal had to fall.

Thus, when Mr. Cardinal began flying at the window in a way almost identical to the obsessive behavior of Mr. Poophead, we were at first *amused*. After all, it afforded us an unusually intimate view of this gorgeous creature. And from the previous experience, I was confident that he wasn't doing any permanent damage to the glass.

Even when we got tired of it and were no longer amused, we saw him more as a misbehaving angel than as anything loathsome.

Unlike the cowbird, however, Mr. Cardinal grew more and more obsessive until his narcissistic lunges were no longer occasional and intermittent, but persistent and constant—from first daylight to sundown. The incessant pecking began around 5:00 A.M. and continued nonstop until 9:00 or so at night. The cardinal song that we had always thought melodious began to remind us of a squeaky seesaw. And as soon as we heard it at the crack of dawn, we knew he was back: *Irpy-irpy, irpy-irpy*— then *thwap* against the window! *Irpy-irpy, irpy-irpy*—thwap! *Irpy-irpy, irpy-irpy*—THWAP! Every thirty seconds or so, sixteen hours a day: *Irpy-irpy, irpy-irpy*—THWAP!

At night we began to anticipate the interrupted sleep like a too-early-set alarm clock. After several days of this, I cut Mr. Cardinal's favorite perching branch off of the hackberry. He changed branches. Two days later, I pruned all the branches on that side of the tree. He switched to the forsythia. I pruned the forsythia. He went back to the hackberry, clinging sideways to its narrow thorny trunk. I cut down the hackberry. He went back to the forsythia. *Irpy-irpy, irpy-irpy*—THWAP! THWAP! THWAP! THWAP! THWAP!

Bobbie called Cornell Extension. They said that this was a known bird behavior that sometimes could be cured by covering the window so that it could no longer see its reflection. We taped newspaper over the window. Mr. Cardinal moved to the next window over, perching on the yew and attacking his reflection in the *center* casement pane. We taped newspaper over that window, too. He moved to the third section. We covered that. He moved to the hawthorn at the window in front of the kitchen sink. We covered *that*. The kitchen was so wrapped in old newspaper that being in it began to make us feel like dead fish.

When all the kitchen windows were draped gruesomely, this cardinal from hell moved to the lilac in front of the tri-part casement window in the *living room!*

By now, half of our downstairs had been newspapered into semidarkness for nearly two weeks.

When Bobbie covered over the living-room window, I told her that this had better work or I was going to shoot it. "If you can," she said, "that would be fine."

The next day Mr. Cardinal moved to the magnolia outside the small window in the bathroom. I went down to Hepler's Hardware and, for the first time in my life, bought a box of ammunition, 12-gauge #6 bird shot.

At home, I got out my antique Fitchburg "Champion" single-shot shotgun—that I had never yet fired.

In fact, I hadn't fired a gun in thirty years, not since I went hunting with a high-school debating partner of mine, a minister's son in South Bend. On that day, I'd wounded a rabbit which I never found—sickening me sufficiently into the realization that hunting was not my thing.

I did know that I was a good shot, however. Eight years or so before my "hunting" experience, as a lonely kid at Camp Eberhart, I'd spent most of my free time at the camp rifle range, earning four marksmanship badges in just two weeks. If I could put eight out of ten .22 slugs in the heart of a bull's-eye at fifty yards, hitting a cardinal with a spray of birdshot at ten or twelve feet did not seem beyond my rusty abilities.

After examining the gun nervously to make sure that the inside of the barrel looked clean, I put a shell in the chamber, snapped the gun shut, then slid open the door to the deck. But as soon as the door moved, the cardinal took off and flew into the woods across the road. Maybe that was the end of it, I hoped.

A few minutes later, though, he was back at his spot. This time I went out the front door and tried to sneak around back, but again, as soon as I peeked around the corner of the house, he flew off instantly. Inside the house, I cracked a window and waited, but somehow he knew I was there—and didn't return until I had closed the window.

Irpy-irpy —THWAP! *Irpy-irpy* —THWAP!

I had not only come to despise this particular bird, but I was coming to dislike the sight and sound of *all* cardinals. How could I have ever thought that *irpy-irpy* was melodious?

All day—at least till Annie got home from school—I played hide-and-seek with him and never got off a shot. Annie, a sophomore in high school, was now a vegetarian and a member of PETA (People for the Ethical Treatment of Animals); I had not told her that I intended to shoot the bird.

The next day, after Bobbie had taken Annie to school and gone on to work, I again positioned myself outside behind the corner of the house and waited. This time, when Mr. Cardinal returned to the magnolia and became so absorbed in his self-defeating task that he didn't see me, I shot him.

One shot, and he dropped like a small red pincushion.

How frighteningly easy it was. The siege was over. I spoke to him and told him I was sorry, but that he'd left me no choice. I put one of his brilliant red tailfeathers in my shirt pocket—and tossed his warm body into the encroaching sprawl of wild raspberries that ran down the slope alongside the yard. Inside, I uncovered the kitchen and living-room windows and let light back into the house. I felt very adult. And that something inside me was very changed.

Harmony had failed. Humor had failed. Tolerance had

failed. This had not been killing an animal for meat or putting down a pet. After all these years of finding alternatives, I had finally brought ammo and gun together—as a solution to something.

· 54 ·
RED SQUIRRELS

After killing Mr. Cardinal, it was a long time before I could look at a cardinal or hear a cardinal song and not feel a bit queasy and mistrustful—as if *this one* might also suddenly charge the window and take up Mr. Cardinal's compulsion, like one soldier replacing another. The same cardinal calls that, for almost all my life, had made me look up with bright expectations now had me seeing red flashes of a different kind; every time I heard *irpy-irpy*—I still kept listening for the THWAP.

I never regretted killing the crazy cardinal. As with the rabid possum I'd once killed with a shovel, what I regretted was the *need* to kill it—that I had run out of options or patience, that the responsible or "necessary" thing should have come to that.

And now that I had finally brought ammunition into the house and used my gun, killing had suddenly become much easier. When, in the face of Elijah's hunting ineptitude, ground-hogs and rabbits got in the garden, shooting them was much easier than redoing the fence, or trying to convince them that whatever we put in a live-trap was more appealing than a raised bed of tender lettuce, peas on a string, luscious rows of newly sprouted beans. In fact, even a rabbit or groundhog *near* the garden became tempting game: Why wait for it to do damage? Turn it into dogfood now and eliminate the middleman.

The problem was not death of a few rabbits, of which there was an inbred surplus; nor even of that eye-narrowing heart-jumping trigger-squeezing moment that matured so easily to craftsmanlike satisfaction; the problem was that once I killed one of something, all the others like it also began to look only like potential pests. Unlike William Blake, I could not so clearly separate my songs of "Innocence" and "Experience." It just wasn't in my nature to feel good about empathizing with Peter Rabbit in the morning and acting like Mr. McGregor in the afternoon.

With no other creatures, though, did this play out quite as disturbingly as with the red squirrels. We've always had a variety of squirrels at our feeders: red squirrels, gray squirrels and chipmunks. They were all wonderful to watch, despite the amount of birdseed that they not only ate, but lardered away. These were not quite the same as city, park, campus and suburban squirrels: lazy, semitame, almost like fat old cats; these were of those same *species*, but—as "country" squirrels which were hunted commonly by hawks, humans and other predators (it was not unusual for us to see a rifle-toting neighbor boy walking on our road with two or three squirrels hanging from his belt)—they remained extremely fit and wary—bolting back to the woods at the cracking of a window or the sound of a coming car.

The exception to this was a decidedly unskittish Manx chipmunk which hung around the house for several winters. We knew it to be the same animal because of its missing tail. At the feeders, we often watched him stuffing his cheeks hour after hour as if it were his *job* to remove every last seed. He couldn't possibly have eaten it all; if he'd eaten even one tenth of what he took he'd have gone off like the *Hindenburg*. He was probably trying to fill up some hollow tree somewhere, and keeping him in feed was as expensive as feeding another dog or cat. In fact, we almost came to look at him as a pet. Unlike a pet, though, we weren't even quite sure when he stopped coming. There was no calling "Hotline" or planting of trees; we just accepted the fact that something had probably gotten him.

For many years we had only gray squirrels and chipmunks at the feeders, but then the red squirrels arrived—one, then one or two, then two or three. They were only about half the size of the gray squirrels and were as cute as anything could be, incredibly quick and acrobatic: chasing each other around and through the hollow middle of the pear tree, racing full speed to the most precarious treetop branches and leaping four or five feet to the shaky top of the next tree over. For several winters we couldn't help loving them—despite the fact that they displaced a number of the birds, and that there wasn't any feeder of ours that they couldn't get into. They could climb a half-inch metal pole. They could walk sideways on glass. They could climb straight down the wire filament of our "squirrel-proof" finch feeder, hang by one rear foot, slide the cap up the wire and dive into the tube of niger seed like Scrooge McDuck diving into a swimming pool full of money. We had no baffle they couldn't baffle—even if it meant, as it sometimes did, chewing a hole into the feeder to get the feed out that way.

But it wasn't the damage to the feeders that drove us to drastic means; it was when we discovered that they'd moved into the house—from the woodshed tunneling through the insulation under the rafters and then into our walls. This was no longer a matter of pesky mischief; suddenly, we had several amazingly acrobatic rat-sized rodents living in our house—where they basically had access to everything but the refrigerator.

At first, with dim hopes, we tried to catch them in a live trap which we baited with shelled peanuts. And, after several unsuccessful attempts . . . we caught one. The first time we'd ever gotten a live trap to work! And before the week was out, we also caught the second and the third. Proud of ourselves, heartened by this humane remedy, we took each of them down Gravel Run Road, releasing it into a thick woods about two miles from the house.

After relocating the third, we thought that was it—but the next day another appeared. And the day after that, there were again *two!* When I managed to trap these two, I took them to another woods even farther away. But two days later, there was a red squirrel on the pear tree. And this time, when we tried to trap it, we caught a sparrow instead. And, after that, each time we reset the trap we caught another bird. And in the woodshed, a red squirrel scampered from a new hole into the house right in front of me.

After several weeks, sick of trapping only birds and unable to think of any other solution, I decided to shoot the one or two remaining squirrels before they could reproduce. While I could barely bring myself do it, physically it was as easy as slamming a door. As soon as I cracked open a kitchen window, the squirrel instantly flashed up to what it took to be a safe spot in the upper limbs of the pear tree, and just waited there for me to sight it in and pull the trigger. The *bang* instantly sent the other squirrel flying to the woods, and I desperately hoped he'd take the message and stay there.

Outside, I picked up the little body and sadly set it in the nearby thicket. Later, Elijah sniffed it out and brought it up on the porch, leaving it on the welcome mat in front of the door. I told myself that I had done all I could. At least we'd saved five of them, and maybe this was the only one I'd have to kill.

The next day, when I saw the other squirrel back at the feeder, I almost screamed. I tried to trap it, but caught only another sparrow. So I shot it.

Two days later, there were two more squirrels on the pear tree! I shot one in the morning and the other in the afternoon. The second body I put in the hollow of the pear tree, hoping that maybe *that* would finally get the message across; but still they kept coming. While the body count piled in my mind, I was committed now; if I stopped and left the job half-done, it would seem as if I'd killed the others for nothing. I began to keep the gun downstairs and the box of shells on the mantle-piece. Over the next several weeks—never missing once—I shot thirteen in all. Then finally they stopped coming.

· 55 ·

LAST SPRING

Two summers ago, my father was diagnosed with lung cancer. He'd undergone several different chemotherapies since then, even though, from the beginning, his oncologist had said that there was little hope. Then, unexpectedly, early the next spring, one of the chemotherapies had an extremely positive effect. A month or so later, the doctor said that my father was in complete remission . . . in fact, had "hit a home run!"

The doctor—almost ready to declare it a "cure"—prescribed seven weeks of radiation treatment "just to be sure—to kill any cancer cells that might be left."

South Bend always had hard winters, usually harder than ours. Not this year, though. Our winter had been extremely tough—and then, on March 13, we got hit by a freak snowstorm—"The Storm of the Century" some called it—39 inches of new snow dumped onto the still-frozen ground.

A few weeks after the blizzard, the weather suddenly turned warm and gorgeous and created the "Flood of the Decade." As high up as we were, we mostly escaped the effects of that, except that our yard and gardens looked like rice paddies, and the barn had sprung leaks in the roof and one foundation wall. On the other hand, the pond was as full as it had ever been. However, when I sloshed down to see if the fish were yet active, I found hundreds of them floating dead on the water.

"Fish kill," it was called. When I called the Conservation Department, I was told that it had happened to a lot of ponds this year. The deep snow had simply deprived the pond plants of sunlight for too long; there had been an insufficient exchange of carbon dioxide and oxygen, and the fish had suffocated.

Although I didn't yet know it, they were *all* dead. I had immediately seen Old Granddad, our only lunker, belly up and deteriorating. But then I saw a *second* lunker, just as big! And a third—and then a fourth! This astounded me because I knew Old Granddad had been the last of the original bass still in the pond. However, when I'd gotten a long branch and floated all four of these large fish within reach, I saw that only one of the lunkers was a bass; the others were *grass carp* —the grass carp that we'd never seen once since first putting them in the pond, and, in the ensuing upheaval, had presumed relegated to bass food. And now they were even larger than Old Granddad— and just as dead.

For several weeks, I continued to haunt the pond in hopes that some of the small bass had survived, but to no avail. However, it was only the fish—and one turtle—that had died. The rest of the pond life, including at least three other turtles, had survived. Not only survived, but with the pond as full as it was and without the bass as competition, most of the pond creatures were flourishing. When, in the warm weather, the frogs came to mate, it was a frog orgy like we'd never seen before. And for the first time we not only had two pairs of mallards on the pond, but four bufflehead ducks as well. And with such a surfeit of frogs, we also had more herons than usual. The boatmen, back swimmers, damselflies and dragonflies abounded. Everything, it seemed, had made it, except the fish and one turtle. Including the leeches.

This year kept coming at us from all angles. In light of my father's illness, the death of the fish had seemed all the more powerful, even symbolically connected in some way that I didn't exactly understand. This was also the first year that both

Zack and Annie were out of the house away at college—Annie a freshman at Yale; Zack, now transferred to UCLA, taking his junior year abroad at Yonsei University in Seoul, Korea, partially paid for by a "Pacific Rim" scholarship—which seemed not only out of the nest, but out of this world.

Also, my job was in the process of ending. For six years, I'd been teaching and counseling for a Keuka College satellite program at the Elmira Correctional Facility, one of New York State's seventeen maximum-security prisons. For me, this had been an intensely satisfying and eye-opening job, but the college—having decided that the program was no longer financially tenable—had decided that this academic year would be their last. I'd been assigned the task of closing the program—and my job—by the end of June.

During spring break—in part to celebrate our twenty-fifth anniversary in April—we went to visit Zack in Korea. We were past due to take an "exotic" trip, and our tickets even afforded us a five-day layover in Hawaii. On the Big Island, we climbed the Kilauea volcano and stared down into the steaming craters of the earth, then drove to a spot where the flowing lava was pushing hot against the sea, cooling to create the land right before our eyes. Then, in Korea, where almost no one could speak to us and we could read nothing, we were like children as Zack shepherded us from place to place, telling us what to eat and where we shouldn't go, taking us to Buddhist temples, the ocean resort in Pusan, the cherry blossom festival in Chinhae.

In May, my father's cough came back. At first the doctor thought it was just a lung burn from the radiation, but then discovered the cancer had not only returned but metastasized. Somehow, for the May weekend of my niece Mandy's *bat mitzvah*, Dad managed to rally, even walk by himself up to the altar and hand the Torah to his granddaughter. But he never really had another good day after that.

I spent a few days with Dad in early June. Seeing the shape he was in, when I came back, I did everything I could to close the prison college program two weeks ahead of schedule. Using the last of my residual personal and vacation days, I went back to South Bend. After two weeks of terrible suffering, my father died on the Fourth of July.

· 56 ·
LAST SUMMER

In mid-May, Annie came home from school. The very next day she was in surgery—a thigh tendon with a button of bone at each end being screwed into her knee to replace the anterior cruciate ligament that she'd damaged two years before—the two previous surgeries and rehabilitative efforts having failed to rid the knee of wobble and pain. Annie was on crutches for her cousin Mandy's *bat mitzvah*, off the crutches but still hobbling at my father's funeral in July.

All of us needing to get back on our feet and move on, we spent the rest of the summer grasping for healing elements: Annie working hard to rehabilitate her knee; Bobbie catching up at work; me writing; both of us losing ourselves in the garden. Even though we'd been late getting the garden in, the right combination of sun and rain got the garden up and going well.

Bobbie also put up two hummingbird feeders, one in the front of the house and the other on the side porch between the copper bell wind chimes and the cascading purple clematis. She'd tried hummingbird feeders before, but had only rarely attracted a hummingbird (more often drawn to her red geraniums than to the red sugar water in the feeders), and we'd never gotten one to hang around. This year, though, at least three hummingbirds came and stayed all summer. Fluttering in place or flashing off, they were almost too quick to focus on or follow, but eventually we realized that we had at least one female because she didn't have a ruby throat. And then we sometimes saw two males at the same time, chasing each other and fighting tiny careering battles in a midair blur. We had always wrongly considered hummingbirds to be too delicate and sweet-natured to be aggressive. I'd also never seen a hummingbird land before, but once they became regulars, we occasionally saw one stop and perch. Whirring and hovering in the air they could have been taken for some gigantic kind of bees, but perched on the branch of a yew or maple they looked only like the small birds they were.

One midsummer day after Annie had rehabbed herself enough to be hobbling around the yard, she saw a hummingbird moth and called me out to see it. She didn't know what she was looking at. In flight it had looked almost exactly like a hummingbird, but, when it had landed on a geranium she'd seen its feathery antennae and minuscule head—and thought it was a hummingbird mutant or something. I knew immediately what it was, but she didn't believe me until I showed her the picture of a hummingbird moth in one of our insect books. Not only was its mimickry amazing, but we also pondered the fact that we'd never seen one until this year, when the hummingbirds had stayed. Did these moths tag along with the hummingbirds, scout around looking for them, or what?

In midsummer, I also decided to drain the pond.

The pond had become unusable, even to me. Not only was it fishless and as weedy and leech-infested as ever, but, because of the thousands of decomposing fish, it stank terribly and was probably contaminated. We decided that it was the perfect time to dredge and deepen it, clear all the weeds and willows and cattails from the roots on up—and, quite possibly, get rid of the leeches, too. Without small children, we were no longer as concerned about keeping the perimeter shallow, and we thought a deeper pond would also inhibit the weeds from coming back so fast.

We knew this would be an unpleasant task. Even with the fish gone, the pond was still a viable ecosystem brimming with creatures that would not survive the process. I'd been too humbled by this year to feel the least bit godlike about causing this Apocalypse and Rebirth; but—in a most human way— after weighing the pros and cons, we concluded that the pond would surely soon be replenished with life and, for our purposes, essentially be renewed.

I bought an irrigation pump at Agway that had 20 feet of intake hose on one end and 30 feet of effluent hose on the other. It was awkward to set up. The intake hose was fitted with a plastic strainer that had to be tied to stay in the bottom of a weighted bucket to keep it from sinking into the muck. Maneuvering the thing was like wrestling with a giant octopus, and it was a bear to prime. But, once going, the two inch hose began pulling out something like 40 or 50 gallons a minute and sending it off down the hill on the other side of the dike. Every two and a half hours I refilled it with gas, restarted it and it was off and running again. For over two weeks it ran like this and, by the time the pond had been reduced to a one- to two-foot puddle—25 or 30 feet in diameter, I estimated that something like a quarter of a million gallons of water had gone over the dike. As the pond diminished, I had to keep moving the pump closer and closer in to the shrinking center of the pond, laying a board walkway across the fresh muck as I went. At the other end, I had to add two sections of extension hose so that the effluent could still reach over the dike. It was a muddy mess, and twice rainstorms refilled the pond enough to make me pull the pump back, and then later begin edging it in again.

Despite the mess, though, I was getting it done and was quite satisfied with myself. In the large area where the water had receded, I could see the damage that the muskrat and groundhog tunnels had slowly been doing to the dike. As the July sun baked the surrounding outer rings of muddy clay, the water-deprived weeds began to wither and die and the pond crater took on an otherworldly, moonscape quality—a look that I found more fascinating than disturbing.

What was disturbing, however, was that, as the pond shrunk, most of the pond creatures kept being forced to move ever more toward the center. Some of the animals—like the frogs and turtles and nesting birds—had long since abandoned their homes and gone elsewhere, but those that were dependent on the water had no choice but to keeping moving inward. All along I knew this was happening, but only gradually did it become horribly unignorable. Fortunately, the water was too murky for me to see all of the various creatures, but the water became so crowded and roiling with life—many of the creatures squirming and leaping at the surface—that the remaining shallow bowl began to look more and more like a large earthen pot of simmering stew.

Then the water became so thick with life that whatever was closest to the center got pushed into the bucket, either clogging the plastic strainer or sucked through it into the intake hose, the effluence turning more and more into a kind of living bouillabaisse—newts, tadpoles, water bugs, boatmen, back swimmers—being spit out in the weedy field behind the dike. The pump was constantly fighting not to gag and quit, and so was I. This horrifying endgame went on for almost two weeks, again twice prolonged by rainstorms that doubled the size of the puddle and forced me to retrace my steps. When the strainer became so clogged with larger creatures that the pump lost its prime, I waded out to unclog it, each step sinking me thigh deep in the muck—the thickness of life dancing against every part of me that touched the water.

Finally, when the water was no more than six or eight inches deep, the diameter of the puddle about seven feet across, the pump was gasping and quitting so often that there was nothing more to be done. I cleaned the pump and hoses and put them in the barn, and hoped that what was left would dry up before the autumn rains. While the center never dried completely, in a month or so the rest of the pond crater became firm enough for Charlie Hill's men to come in with bulldozer and front loader and proceed to dredge and deepen the pond according to plan.

The horror of draining the pond stayed with me for quite a while, but at least we also soon had a new pond waiting to fill. Even so, I knew that if the pond was ever to be drained again, it would be done by some future owner of this land, not by me.

· 57 ·
LAST FALL

Last fall Bobbie found a sister. A half-sister named Diana, whom she'd known about but had not seen for almost thirty-five years. Like *Rashomon*, this story had several different, sometimes conflicting versions, but the way Bobbie'd learned it was this: As a teenager, Bobbie's mother had been sent to America from Bulgaria in order to find and marry an older man who would take care of her, which she'd done. After something like three miserable years, however, she'd taken their daughter and left him. But he had gotten the police to snatch the girl back and then had taken her to somewhere in Ohio. After some corresponding, visiting, several moves, unsuccessful legal attempts and depletion of resources, Vera had either lost track of Diana or, in despondency, had simply given up. Clearly, though, she had finally pulled back, turned the page, and given up on trying to make any further contact. Later, as a young woman, Diana had sought her mother out; but, for whatever reasons, they hadn't gotten along and had again become estranged.

Now, though, thirty-some years later, by freak coincidence Bobbie's sister Gigi in Seattle had come across one of Diana's daughters. Soon after that, Gigi had visited her lost sister in Vancouver, and together they had planned a grand reunion for all the women in the family at the end of September.

For weeks, as Bobbie both looked forward to and was emotionally wrenched by thoughts of this reunion and all it dredged up, Shiver had reached his last legs. Because of all that Bobbie was dealing with, I offered to put Shiver down while she was in Seattle, a task that we'd both been dreading for some time.

For several years, Shiver had been expanding from a benign slow-growing tumor that had steadily distended his middle—causing him no real pain, only more and more to waddle and flop—which, for quite a while, had seemed only slightly to exaggerate his normally phlegmatic personality. Early on, the vet told us that we could subject him to expensive and extremely unpromising surgery, though at his age she didn't recommend it. So we'd just let it go. But by this summer, it had gotten so bad that he had to claw his way up to a footstool or lap and could only push himself from place to place, looking like an orange-and-white circus balloon with paws painted on it. Though still in no obvious pain, he was also mostly deaf and senile, and could no longer use the cat box even when we put down a flat cookie sheet that he didn't have to climb into. He *tried*, poor thing, but he was leaking all over the place and after a while the whole area had become bleached and stinking with urine.

It was simply time.

We didn't want to put him down while Annie was still home, though. But we told her to say good-bye to him and, after she had returned to school and Bobbie was in Seattle, I took him.

As with Star, Shiver hated the vet, and detested even the sight of the cat carrier. And, as before, I thought it would have be much kinder to just give him a can of tuna, put him out in the sun, and sneak up behind him—he'd go out in happy cat dreams and never know what hit him. Again, though, I couldn't do it—and so I took him down. When I'd finally calmed him on the vet's table, he even started purring.

At home, after burying him and planting a tree over him (another little wild snippet from Annie's tree), I got out the Lysol and Mr. Clean and scrubbed away most of the cat-urine smell, doing my best to remind myself that people are animals but animals are not people.

When Bobbie came back, for the first time we began to feel like empty-nesters. Not only were Zack and Annie far afield, but it was the first time since Bobbie and I had known each other that there wasn't at least one animal in the house.

EPILOGUE:
LAST WINTER/THIS SPRING

The years go by so fast, and yet so many things can happen in a year; some years can drain your heart and refill it, again and again. Like last year, season by season bursting and repairing its seams. The winter was also hard: fourteen major storms, many days of record cold and record amounts of snow. From the first day of winter to the first day of spring, there wasn't a single day when we could see the ground.

Even so, the heavy snows had been good for refilling the pond. We couldn't wait to see it come alive again, reseed the area around it, see if we'd actually gotten rid of the leeches, see if it might return to the pristine and delightful entity it had once been. We'd already decided not to stock the fish for a while, but just see what kind of habitat the pond would develop on its own.

And we'd already gotten our garden seeds, having decided to plant early and take our chances.

I'd also gotten Bobbie two bluebird houses which we were itching to set up and see if bluebirds would actually come.

And ever since Shiver's demise, we'd been talking about getting a kitten as soon as the weather broke. The other day, when we talked on the phone to Annie, she said she'd heard that it was always better to get two, so they could keep each other company.

We said we'd just have to see about that.